Proverbs 1-9

Wise Up and Live

D1552847

JOHN A. STEWART

Lamplighters International is an evangelical Christian ministry that helps people engage with God and His Word and equips believers to be disciple-makers.

For additional information about Lamplighters ministry resources, contact:

Lamplighters International
771 NE Harding Street, Suite 250
Minneapolis, MN USA 55413
or visit our website at
www.LamplightersUSA.org

Product Code Pr1-NK-2P

ISBN # 978-1-931372-45-9

CONTENTS

How to Use This Study

WHAT IS LAMPLIGHTERS?

Lamplighters is a Christian ministry that helps individuals engage with God and His Word and equips believers to be disciple-makers. This Bible study, comprising ten individual lessons, is a self-contained unit and an integral part of the entire discipleship ministry. When you have completed the study, you will have a much greater understanding of a portion of God's Word, with many new truths that you can apply to your life.

HOW TO STUDY A LAMPLIGHTERS LESSON

A Lamplighters study begins with prayer, your Bible, the weekly lesson, and a sincere desire to learn more about God's Word. The questions are presented in a progressive sequence as you work through the study material. You should not use Bible commentaries or other reference books (except a dictionary) until you have completed your weekly lesson and met with your weekly group. Approaching the Bible study in this way allows you to personally encounter many valuable spiritual truths from the Word of God.

To gain the most out of the Bible study, find a quiet place to complete your weekly lesson. Each lesson will take approximately 45–60 minutes to complete. You will likely spend more time on the first few lessons until you are familiar with the format, and our prayer is that each week will bring the discovery of important life principles.

The writing space within the weekly studies provides the opportunity for you to answer questions and respond to what you have learned. Putting answers in your own words, and including Scripture references where appropriate, will help you personalize and commit to memory the truths you have learned. The answers to the questions will be found in the Scripture references at the end of each question or in the passages listed at the beginning of each lesson.

If you are part of a small group, it's a good idea to record the specific dates that you'll be meeting to do the individual lessons. Record the specific dates each time the group will be meeting next to the lesson titles on the Contents page. Additional lines have been provided for you to record when you go through this same study at a later date.

The side margins in the lessons can be used for the spiritual insights you glean from other group or class members. Recording these spiritual truths will likely be a spiritual help to you and others when you go through this study again in the future.

AUDIO INTRODUCTION

A brief audio introduction is available to help you learn about the historical background of the book, gain an understanding of its theme and structure, and be introduced to some of the major truths. Audio introductions are available for all Lamplighters studies and are a great resource for the group leader; they can also be used to introduce the study to your group. To access the audio introductions, go to www.LamplightersUSA.org.

"DO YOU THINK?" QUESTIONS

Each weekly study has a few *"do you think?"* questions designed to help you to make personal applications from the biblical truths you are learning. In the first lesson the *"do you think?"* questions are placed in italic print for easy identification. If you are part of a study group, your insightful answers to these questions could be a great source of spiritual encouragement to others.

PERSONAL QUESTIONS

Occasionally you'll be asked to respond to personal questions. If you are part of a study group you may choose not to share your answers to these questions with the others. However, be sure to answer them for your own benefit because they will help you compare your present level of spiritual maturity to the biblical principles presented in the lesson.

A FINAL WORD

Throughout this study the masculine pronouns are frequently used in the generic sense to avoid awkward sentence construction. When the pronouns *he*, *him*, and *his* are used in reference to the Trinity (God the Father, Jesus Christ, and the Holy Spirit), they always refer to the masculine gender.

This Lamplighters study was written after many hours of careful preparation. It is our prayer that it will help you "… grow in the grace and knowledge of our Lord and Savior Jesus Christ. To Him be the glory both now and forever. Amen" (2 Peter 3:18).

WHAT IS AN INTENTIONAL DISCIPLESHIP BIBLE STUDY?

THE *NEXT STEP* IN BIBLE STUDY

The Lamplighters Bible study series is ideal for individual, small group, and classroom use. This Bible study is also designed for Intentional Discipleship training. An Intentional Discipleship (ID) Bible study has four key components. Individually they are not unique, but together they form the powerful core of the ID Bible study process.

1. Objective: Lamplighters is a discipleship training ministry that has a dual objective: (1) to help individuals engage with God and His Word and (2) to equip believers to be disciple-makers. The small group format provides extensive opportunity for ministry training, and it's not limited by facilities, finances, or a lack of leadership staffing.

2. Content: The Bible is the focus rather than Christian books. Answers to the study questions are included within the study guides, so the theology is in the study material, not in the leader's mind. This accomplishes two key objectives: (1) It gives the group leader confidence to lead another individual or small group without fear, and (2) it protects the small group from theological error.

3. Process: The ID Bible study process begins with an Open House, which is followed by a 6–14-week study, which is followed by a presentation of the Final Exam (see graphic on page 8). This process provides a natural environment for continuous spiritual growth and leadership development.

4. Leadership Development: As group participants grow in Christ, they naturally invite others to the groups. The leader-trainer (1) identifies and recruits new potential leaders from within the group, (2) helps them register for online discipleship training, and (3) provides in-class leadership mentoring until they are both competent and confident to lead a group according to the ID Bible study process. This leadership development process is scalable, progressive, and comprehensive.

OVERVIEW OF THE LEADERSHIP TRAINING AND DEVELOPMENT PROCESS

There are three stages of leadership training in the Intentional Discipleship process: (1) leading studies, (2) training leaders, and (3) multiplying groups (see appendix for greater detail).

Intentional Discipleship
Training & Development Process

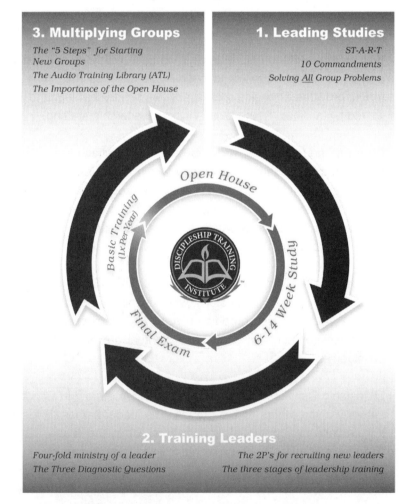

3. Multiplying Groups

The "5 Steps" for Starting New Groups
The Audio Training Library (ATL)
The Importance of the Open House

1. Leading Studies

ST-A-R-T
10 Commandments
Solving All Group Problems

Open House

Basic Training (1x Per Year)

Final Exam

6-14 Week Study

2. Training Leaders

Four-fold ministry of a leader
The Three Diagnostic Questions

The 2P's for recruiting new leaders
The three stages of leadership training

How Can I Be Trained?

Included within this Bible study is the student workbook for Level 1 (Basic Training). Level 1 training is both free and optional. Level 1 training teaches you a simple 4-step process (ST-A-R-T) to help you prepare a life-changing Bible study and 10 proven small group leadership principles that will help your group thrive. To register for a Level 1 online training event, either as an individual or as a small group, go to www.LamplightersUSA.org/training or www.discipleUSA. org. If you have additional questions, you can also call 800-507-9516.

Introduction

Many Christians believe the book of Proverbs is the most helpful book in the Bible. The book offers valuable instruction on a wide variety of subjects such as personal conduct, interpersonal relationships, work, money management, effective communication, emotional health, and business and personal ethics. The practical teaching in Proverbs has inspired many people to read the chapter of Proverbs that corresponds with the day of the month.

A casual reading of the book of Proverbs, however, offers no magical cure for those who are looking for practical answers in life. The proverbs must be studied carefully if we are to comprehend their unique nature and meaning and unearth their rich spiritual truths. Even the book of Proverbs itself warns us: **Like a thorn that goes into the hand of a drunkard is a proverb in the mouth of fools** (Proverbs 26:9).

Background

The Hebrew Bible, the Old Testament scriptures, is divided into three sections: the Law, the Writings, and the Prophets. Proverbs is found in the section known as the Writings. The book of Proverbs is also part of a smaller classification of Scripture known as *wisdom literature*. Wisdom literature is characterized by a strong emphasis on the practical aspects of life, frequent use of questions, and a repetitious appeal for man to evaluate his life goals and conduct during his earthly existence. The books of Job, Ecclesiastes, and a few of the psalms fill out this group. In the New Testament, the book of James is often included in wisdom literature.

Bible scholars believe the proverbs were originally taught to the young men of Israel during a period of relative peace to help them understand the importance of exercising wisdom in daily living. The absence of war, or its imminent threat, often led people to adopt a superficial approach toward life, and the instruction of Proverbs was an appeal to young Jewish men to choose the path of wisdom.

Proverbs is comprised of several sections written at various times and involving several writers (Proverbs 1:1; 10:1; 25:1; 30:1; 31:1). King Solomon reigned from 971 to -931 BC, and King Hezekiah reigned from 729 to 686 BC. This has convinced many Bible scholars to believe that the compilation of Proverbs was completed around 700 B.C. (assuming Agur and Lemuel wrote before then).

What Is a Proverb?

The title comes from the opening phrase, "The proverbs of Solomon" (Proverbs 1:1). The Hebrew word translated "proverb" is *mashal*, which has the root meaning "to be like" or "to represent." Our English word *proverb* comes from two Latin roots, *pro* meaning "for" and *verb,* which means "word." Biblical proverbs are short wisdom maxims or truisms that offer practical instruction consistent with God's moral order of life. They were written in a variety of literary forms (see the following section) to instruct God's people regarding right conduct and character in the spiritual, moral, and social realms of life. Proverbs should not be interpreted as absolute universal laws or unconditional promises (Proverbs 26:4–5).

Literary Form

The first nine chapters of the book are mainly a series of fatherly exhortations to the speaker's son, encouraging him to accept wisdom as the essential possession of life. The actual proverbs begin in chapter 10, where the two-line proverbs become dominant.

The proverbs are categorized by their various forms.
a. Connecting Proverbs (synonymous parallelism). This is one of the simplest types of proverbs, in which two similar ideas are expressed in different words, often linked by the word *and* (Proverbs 11:25).
b. Contrasting Proverbs (antithetical parallelism). In this type of proverb the first line is contrasted in the second, and the word *but* is often used to set off the contrast (Proverbs 10:1).
c. Completing Proverbs (synthetic parallelism). In this type of proverb the second line completes or develops the idea of the first line (Proverbs 15:30).
d. Cultural Proverbs (parabolic parallelism). This proverb explains its ethical object by a resemblance drawn from the realm of natural and everyday life (Proverbs 27:15).

Theme

The resounding theme of the book of Proverbs is wisdom—God's wisdom. Proverbs tells what wisdom is, the price you must pay to gain wisdom, where to find wisdom, the price you will pay if you reject wisdom, and how a wise person navigates through the various situations of life. The words *wise* and *wisdom* occur more than 125 times in Proverbs.

God has created the world according to His moral order and His creation, and though it is marred by the fall of man, it still functions according to His creative design. The book of Proverbs gives man practical instruction about how he can live in harmony with God's plan. Author Warren Wiersbe says, "The wise person believes there is a God, that He is the Creator and Ruler of all things, and that He has put within His creation a divine order that, if obeyed, leads ultimately to success." Success is not the acquisition of material goods and position but the consistent union of God and man in one eternal cooperative effort that brings glory to God and divine favor to man.

So Where Is Jesus Christ?

The Bible is more than a moral and ethical handbook—something that educates and inspires man to redouble his efforts to fulfill God's plan for his life. Rightly understood, the Word of God, including Proverbs, leads men to the realization that, without salvation in Jesus Christ, they are completely helpless to live out God's plan for their lives. The apostle Paul told Timothy that the holy scriptures (including Proverbs) are able to **make you wise for salvation through faith which is in Christ Jesus** (2 Timothy 3:15).

God's Word gives man His plan for wise living. Jesus Christ died on the cross to give man salvation so he can comprehend and live according to the Father's plan. The Holy Spirit gives man the power to live out His plan, and Jesus Christ is the perfect example of a person who lived His life according to the wisdom of God.

Importance of This Study

The book of Proverbs has been applicable to believers in every age, but it is particularly relevant to our society. Peace and prosperity offer us a myriad of choices and the false assurance that money and power are the keys to happiness. The wisdom of Proverbs warns us against becoming hapless victims of folly's deceit. Instead, we are to be willing recipients of the wisdom of God. Proverbs sets in antithesis the path to destruction and the path to wise and abundant living.

Unfortunately, the victims of folly's deceit are no longer faceless names presented antiseptically in the media. They are too often friends, neighbors, coworkers, and family members. Can this tragedy of human destruction be stopped? Wisdom answers affirmatively as she shouts in the streets, lifting up her voice in the square (Proverbs 1:20) and calling to all who will listen. The voice we hear in the square is the wisdom of Proverbs.

ONE

KNOWLEDGE AND WISDOM

Read Introduction, Proverbs 1:1–7; other references as given.

The key word in Proverbs is *wisdom*. The Hebrew word for wisdom (*hokmah*) means "the ability to live life skillfully." It is the way of thinking, including decision making, and living that separates the wise man from the fool. Proverbs contains a collection of a father's exhortations to his son and other children to gain wisdom (chapters 1–9), with sayings and instruction for wise and effective living (chapters10–31). The book of Proverbs is God's instruction manual on living a life that is honoring to God and honorable before other people.

In this first lesson, you will learn that wisdom is available to all (James 1:5), but not everyone is willing to receive it. You will also learn the difference between knowledge and wisdom. And as you learn about wisdom, you will naturally examine your life to see whether you are living skillfully in all areas of your life.

Before you begin this lesson and each lesson in this study, ask God to reveal Himself through His precious Word and to transform you into the image of His Son. May God bless your diligent study of God's Word.

Lombardi Time Rule:

If the leader arrives early, he or she has time to pray, prepare the room, and greet others personally.

ADD GROUP INSIGHTS BELOW

1. a. What is wisdom? Try to answer *without* looking at a dictionary.

Common sense

b. What is your definition of knowledge?

_____

_____

_____

c. What *do you think* is the difference, if any, between knowledge and wisdom?

_____

_____

_____

2. People look to various sources for the truth to guide their lives. Some let their consciences be their guide, but man's conscience can become callous and ineffective because of sin (1 Timothy 4:2). Others let their feelings, intuition, and impressions direct them, but mysticism is always subjective and often misleading. Others rely on their friends, family, and people they admire, but their advice can be contradictory and faulty. Some look within to human reason and common sense to guide them through life, but the Bible warns us: **There is a way that seems right to a man, but its end is the way of death** (Proverbs 14:12).

a. Take a minute to examine how you make decisions. Where do you look for answers to life?

_____

_____

_____

b. What three things must a person do to demonstrate that he has acquired the wisdom of God (James 1:5–6; 3:13; 2 Timothy 3:15)?

_____

_____ (_____).

_____

_____ (_____).

_____

_____ (_____).

Zip-It Rule:

Group members
should agree to
disagree, but
should never be
disagreable.

ADDITIONAL
INSIGHTS

3. God's Word is like a flawless diamond. Each time its pages are turned it reveals another aspect of God's divine nature and His matchless plan for your life. If you embrace the truth, God will reveal more of Himself and His wisdom to you (John 14:21), and you will be transformed into the image of Jesus Christ. You will gain wisdom, peace, and joy, which will enable you to bring glory to His name. What are some practical topics addressed in the book of Proverbs (see Introduction)?

1. _____

2. _____

3. _____

4. _____

5. _____

6. _____

4. The misinterpretation of God's Word has birthed many false religions and cults and brought ruination to countless lives. To avoid being deceived by false teachers, believers should diligently study the Bible. To what does the Bible compare a proverb when it is misused by a fool (Proverbs 26:9)?

_____

_____

5. The Bible is God's inerrant and inspired revelation to man that equips him with everything he needs to honor and obey the Lord. The Old Testament Scriptures were originally written in Hebrew and Aramaic, and the New Testament was written in Greek. List the three major sections or divisions of

the Old Testament and circle the one in which the book of Proverbs is found (see Introduction).

1. _____

2. _____

3. _____

6. Who is the only one who lived his entire life according to the wisdom of God?

   _____

7. Now that you have gained a better understanding of the background of the book of Proverbs, let's study the book itself. List six benefits that a Christian can gain by studying and applying the wisdom of Proverbs 1:2–6.

   _____

   _____

   _____ (v.____).

   _____

   _____

   _____ (v.____).

   _____

   _____

   _____ (v.____).

   _____

   _____

   _____ (v.____).

   _____

   _____

   _____ (v.____).

   _____

_____

_____ (v.____).

Online
Training:

Want to learn
how to lead a
life-changing
Bible study or
start another
study? Go to www.
Lamplighters
USA.org/training
to learn how.

_____

ADDITIONAL
INSIGHTS

8. The Bible says **All Scripture is given by inspiration of God, and is profitable for doctrine** (how to live right), **for reproof** (how to know where you went wrong), **for correction** (how to get back on the right track), **for instruction in righteousness** (how to stay on the right path) (2 Timothy 3:16).

    a. The Bible will help everyone who studies it humbly and thoroughly. What three groups of people will receive specific instruction from the study of Proverbs (Proverbs 1:4–5)?

        1. _____

        2. _____

        3. _____

    b. What *do you think* is the difference between the **simple** and the **young man** (Proverbs 1:4)?

        _____

        _____

        _____

        _____

9. **A wise man will hear and increase learning, ... but fools despise wisdom and instruction** (Proverbs 1:5, 7). What specific things are you doing to gain wisdom and increase your learning about God and His ways so you can bring more glory to His name?

    _____

    _____

    _____

    _____

10. What is the very first step a person must take to gain the knowledge and wisdom of God (Proverbs 1:7)?

_____

_____

What *do you think* this means?

_____

_____

_____

_____

_____

11. a. Hopefully you have learned from this lesson that wisdom (the ability to live life skillfully) is available to all people (James 1:5). In what areas of your life do you see yourself living wisely? Circle your answers.

Personal Life	Family	Work
Leisure	Finances	Relationship(s)
Thoughts	Forgiveness	

   b. In what areas of your life do you see yourself relying on your own reasoning rather than God's wisdom?

Personal Life	Family	Work
Leisure	Finances	Relationship(s)
Thoughts	Forgiveness	

Two

Two Voices Are Calling

**Read Proverbs 1:8–33;
other references as given.**

In the first lesson you learned that there is a difference between knowledge and wisdom. You also learned that the fear of the Lord is the beginning of wisdom, and wisdom enables an individual to live skillfully. God promises wisdom to all who diligently seek it, but fools are fools because they reject God's wisdom. Finally, you examined your own life to see if there are any areas in which you need to live more wisely.

In this lesson you will learn that there are two voices calling in life—the voice of folly (Proverbs 1:8–19) and the voice of wisdom (Proverbs 1:20–33). The voice you listen to will lead you into either the path of skillful living or the path of folly and destruction. And the voices (people) you allow to speak into your life will greatly influence your life. The Bible says **Do not be deceived: "Evil company corrupts good habits"** (1 Corinthians 15:33). This lesson will help you learn how to recognize these two voices and how to listen to the one that leads to life.

Now ask God to reveal Himself to you through His Word and to transform you into the image of His Son.

Volunteer Rule:

If the leader asks for volunteers to read, pray, and answer the questions, group members will be more inclined to invite newcomers.

ADD GROUP
INSIGHTS BELOW

1. Many people are confused about who is primarily responsible for rearing children. Is it the parents' responsibility, the government's responsibility, or the community's responsibility? Others believe children should be left to decide for themselves and the only responsibility of parents is to provide a safe, loving environment in which

children can make their own choices. However, the Bible says, **Foolishness is tangled up in the heart of a youth** (Proverbs 22:15 HCSB).

a. To whom has God given the responsibility of instructing the children (**My son**) regarding the various aspects of wise or skillful living (Proverbs 1:8; Deuteronomy 6:4–8; Ephesians 6:1–4)?

_____

_____

_____

b. If you are a parent, what specific things are you doing to fulfill this important God-given responsibility?

1. _____

2. _____

3. _____

4. _____

If you are single and possibly contemplating marriage in your future, do you think it is important for a potential spouse to make a commitment to assume this God-given responsibility before marriage?
Why?

_____

_____

_____

_____

2. Portions of the Bible were written in metaphorical language. A metaphor is a figure of speech that compares one thing to another to help the listener understand the original thought or idea more fully. For example, Jesus compared how His listeners received His teaching to four types of soil (Mark

4:3–9). In Proverbs 1:9 the Bible compares godly parental instruction to a garland or graceful ornament on a young person's head and chains around their neck. What do you think the use of this metaphor is trying to teach you about godly instruction?

_____

_____

_____

_____

3. The Hebrew words for **simple** (Proverbs 1:4) and **entice** (Proverbs 1:10) come from the same Hebrew root (*pathah*), which means "to be open or spacious." When referring to a person, it means "to be open to any opinion/perspective or uncommitted."

a. Look closely at the meaning of the Hebrew root for "simple" and "entice." Describe as accurately as you can the type of person who is particularly susceptible to the voice of evil and folly (Proverbs 1:4, 7, 10)?

_____

_____

_____

b. Give four characteristics of the sinners who prey on the uncommitted (Proverbs 1:10–19).

1. _____

_____ (v.____).

2. _____

_____ (v.____).

3. _____

_____ (v.____).

59:59 Rule:

Participants appreciate when the leader starts and finishes the studies on time—all in one hour (the 59:59 rule). If the leader doesn't complete the entire lesson, the participants will be less likely to do their weekly lessons and the Bible study discussion will tend to wander.

ADDITIONAL INSIGHTS

4. _____

_____ (v._____).

c. What two groups or individuals are harmed by their sin (Proverbs 1:11, 18–19)?

1. _____ (v._____).

2. _____ (v._____).

4. a. The primary motive of these fools' sin is a financial gain (Proverbs 1:13). What are some examples of sinful attacks on the innocent and unsuspecting that are motivated by a desire for financial advantage?

_____

_____

_____

_____

_____

b. What arguments do fools use to entice the naive and the foolish (Proverbs 1:10–14)?

1. _____

_____ (v._____).

2. _____

_____(v._____).

3. _____

_____ (v._____).

4. _____

_____ (v._____).

5. A smart man learns from his own mistakes, a wise man learns from the mistakes of others, but a fool learns from neither. List at least two reasons the father gives his son

to encourage him to resist sin's enticement (Proverbs 1:10–19)?

1. _____

_____ (v._____).

2. _____

_____ (v._____).

35% Rule:

If the leader talks more than 35% of the time, the group members will be less likely to participate.

ADDITIONAL INSIGHTS

6. In Proverbs 1:20–21 wisdom is personified (another figure of speech) as a woman, lifting up her voice in the open square and crying at the head of the noisy streets and at the gates of the city.

a. What does this imagery teach about wisdom and its availability?

_____

_____

b. What mental picture or image comes into your mind when you think of wisdom lifting up her voice and crying at the head of the noisy streets?

_____

_____

_____

c. Take a minute to review the Hebrew root meaning of the words translated **simple** and **entice** (see question #3). Now restate the first question in Proverbs 1:22 in your own words.

_____

_____

_____

d. What specific spiritual commitments do you think you (and every Christian) should make to avoid becoming a gullible victim of evil men and women?

_____

_____

_____

7. There are several serious consequences of refusing wisdom's call. List at least three (Proverbs 1:24–33).

   1. _____

      _____

      _____ (v.____).

   2. _____

      _____

      _____ (v.____).

   3. _____

      _____

      _____ (v.____).

8. Danger lies ahead for those who refuse the voice of wisdom. Many people, including countless Christians, reject God's appeal and pay the consequences for their folly. In times of trouble, however, some turn to God but find that wisdom will not answer a fool in the day of his calamity (Proverbs 1:24–31).

   a. The New Testament writer James tells us that God gives wisdom **to all liberally and without reproach** (James 1:5). How can God's promise to give wisdom to all men and the warning of Proverbs 1:24–31 to not be available in times of trouble both be true?

      _____

      _____

      _____

b. Why do so many people reject the wisdom of God (Mark 4:14–19; John 3:19; 1 Corinthians 2:14; Hebrews 4:2)?

_____

_____

_____

_____

_____

c. In what areas of your life, if any, do you find yourself rejecting the wisdom of God?

_____

_____

_____

_____

_____

ADDITIONAL INSIGHTS

ADDITIONAL INSIGHTS

THREE

THE VALUE OF WISDOM

Read Proverbs 2; other references as given.

In the previous lesson, you learned that there are two voices calling in life—the voice of wisdom and the voice of folly. Those who are naïve or gullible are particularly susceptible to folly's enticement, with its hollow promises of easy gain and social acceptance. But the voice of wisdom also calls out in the streets and the open squares. Those who seek life recognize her voice and enter her paths of freedom.

In this lesson you'll learn that the grand plans we announce are not as important as the daily decisions we make. For it is the daily decisions, sometimes small and apparently insignificant, that often direct our earthly destiny. A wise decision that many Christians make is to seek the voice of wisdom through the daily reading and study of God's Word. In this lesson you will learn how to establish a time of daily Bible reading and study and the joy you'll receive if you do.

Now ask God to reveal Himself to you through His Word and transform you into the image of Jesus Christ.

Focus Rule:

If the leader helps the group members focus on the Bible, they will gain confidence to study God's Word on their own.

———

ADD GROUP INSIGHTS BELOW

1. The first nine chapters of Proverbs are a series of sermons or fatherly talks on the value of gaining wisdom, which apply to everyone who wants to live skillfully. The first use of the phrase **my son** (Proverbs 1:8) begins the father's first exhortation. The frequent use of the phrase **my son** (e.g., Proverbs 3:11, 21; 4:10, 20; 5:1; 6:1, 3, 20; 7:1) reveals the extent of the father's longing to have his son fully embrace

the path of wisdom and the Father's longing for all believers to embrace it as well.

a. What do you think are the **words** and **commandments** in Proverbs 2:1?

_____

_____

b. Why do you think the father would refer to wisdom as *my* **words** and *my* **commandments** if all wisdom comes from God (Proverbs 2:1)?

_____

_____

_____

_____

2. The word **treasure** (Proverbs 2:1; NIV: "store up") teaches an important spiritual truth that every Christian must understand before he or she can acquire the wisdom of God. What is this?

_____

_____

_____

3. Do you think the words **ear, heart,** and **voice** (Proverbs 2:2–3) represent various religious duties (listening, meditating on Scripture, praying) that must be done to acquire wisdom, or is the writer simply saying that man's total being must become fully engaged in this endeavor (Proverbs 2:2–5)? Why?

_____

_____

_____

4. a. An important two-word phrase, repeated three times in Proverbs 2:1–4, identifies another key to gaining the wisdom of God. What is this important two-word phrase?

_____ _____

b. What does this important phrase teach about acquiring the wisdom of God?

_____

_____

_____

_____

Drawing Rule:

To learn how to draw everyone into the group discussion without calling on anyone, go to www.Lamplighters USA.org/training.

———

ADDITIONAL INSIGHTS

5. In the Western world silver is not considered as precious as gold. In the Old Testament, however, silver is mentioned before gold (except for Deuteronomy and Chronicles), indicating its superior value to the ancient Israelites. Silver was also considered a standard for business transactions and weighed out for payment of purchases and wages. Restate Proverbs 2:4 in your own words, substituting two modern words for **silver** and **hidden treasures** or gold.

_____

_____

_____

_____

6. There are eight spiritual commitments a believer must make before he can truly acquire the knowledge and wisdom of God (Proverbs 2:1–4). The knowledge and wisdom referred to in Proverbs are not the grace-given, God-imparted knowledge of sin (Holy-Spirit conviction) that leads to salvation (2 Timothy 3:15). Wisdom, as it is presented in Proverbs, must be diligently pursued if the Christian wants to comprehend God's will for his life. In what ways do you think an understanding of how man is saved and how he

gains wisdom for daily living should impact a believer's life?

_____

_____

_____

_____

7. a. Solomon listed eight prerequisites for gaining wisdom (Proverbs 2:1–4) before enumerating the blessings of possessing it (Proverbs 2:5–22). In what ways does the word **then** (Proverbs 2:5, 9) affect the promises of blessing in Proverbs 2:5–12?

_____

_____

_____

b. Some view the daily study of God's Word as an academic pursuit devoid of any practical benefit. "After all," they say, "I already know the stories of the Bible." Name at least seven practical benefits you will gain from the diligent study of God's Word (Proverbs 2:5–16).

1. _____

_____ (v._____).

2. _____

_____ (v._____).

3. _____

_____ (v._____).

4. _____

_____ (v._____).

5. _____

_____ (v._____).

6. _____

_____ (v._____).

7. _____

_____ (v._____).

Has your group become a "Holy huddle?" Learn how to reach out to others by taking online leadership training.

————

ADDITIONAL INSIGHTS

c. If you pursue God through a diligent study of His Word, knowledge will become pleasant to your soul (Proverbs 2:10). What important truths does this passage teach about your initial and continuing relationship to wisdom (Proverbs 2:1–10)?

_____

_____

_____

_____

8. There is an excellent definition of wisdom in the parallelism of Proverbs 2:6. What is it?

_____

_____

_____

9. If you seek wisdom with all your heart, discretion will preserve and protect you (Proverbs 2:11). The definition of discretion includes the ability to accurately evaluate multiple options in life and to choose the best one (Proverbs 2:12).

a. List two groups or individuals that wisdom will protect you from falling prey to their solicitations (Proverbs 2:11–16).

_____

_____

b. One of the ways you can discern between wise and wicked men is by evaluating their speech (Proverbs 2:12, 17). Name two speech patterns of ungodly people

33

that prove they don't know the path of uprightness (Proverbs 2:11–16).

1. _____

_____

2. _____

_____

c. List several examples of ungodly or perverse speech you have heard in the past three months.

1. _____

_____

2. _____

_____

3. _____

_____

4. _____

_____

5. _____

_____

6. _____

_____

d. What personal decisions do you think a Christian should make to avoid this verbal contamination?

_____

_____

_____

10. In Proverbs 2:16–19 we see a vivid example of one whose ways are crooked and who lives in darkness. The immoral woman or adulteress (Hebrew *zarah*; the adulteress is

representative of all immoral people, both men and women) is estranged from the corporate life of Israel because of her immoral conduct. What two persons has she broken covenant with (Proverbs 2:17)?

_____

_____

_____

_____

_____

ADDITIONAL INSIGHTS

Four

Wisdom Will Guide You

Read Proverbs 3; other references as given.

In the previous lesson you learned that there are eight prerequisites before you can truly acquire God's wisdom. You also learned that personal Bible study becomes a real joy when we learn to seek God. Lastly, you learned how to recognize ungodly people by their perverse speech.

In this lesson you'll discover that there is a close relationship between right thinking (the wisdom of God) and right living. You will also learn what it means to **lean not on your own understanding** and how to **acknowledge [God] in all your ways** (Proverbs 3:5–6).

Now ask God to reveal Himself to you through His Word and transform you into the image of Jesus Christ.

Gospel Gold Rule:

Try to get all the answers to the questions—not just the easy ones. Go for the gold.

ADD GROUP INSIGHTS BELOW

1. There is an old American proverb that reads, "Sow a thought, reap a habit; sow a habit, reap a lifestyle, sow a lifestyle, reap a destiny [on earth]." When a person says, "I can't help what I think. That's just how I feel", the person is failing to realize that his feelings are merely the emotional extension of his thoughts. If someone is having trouble with "runaway feelings" (fear, anger, unforgiveness, lust, etc.), he should yield himself and his thoughts to God, and right feelings will eventually follow. The apostle Paul said, **[Cast] down arguments and every high thing that exalts itself against the knowledge of God, bringing every thought**

into captivity to the obedience of Christ (2 Corinthians 10:5)

a. In Proverbs 3:1 the father continues his appeal for the son to gain wisdom. What do you think parents can learn about child rearing from the repetition of the phrase **my son** and the father's constant appeal to his son to gain wisdom, especially as it relates to encouraging them to follow the voice of wisdom and reject the voice of folly?

_____

_____

_____

_____

b. If you are a child or teen still living under your parents' authority, how does this passage help you understand their role of instructing you?

_____

_____

_____

_____

2. In Proverbs 3:1–10 there are five proverbial or general promises (Proverbs 3:2, 4, 6, 8, 10). The first, second, and fifth should not be interpreted as absolute promises (see Ecclesiastes 7:15; Isaiah 53:2–3; John 1:11; 1 Corinthians 4:9–12). Each one is preceded by a human obligation that must be met before the anticipated benefit can be realized (Proverbs 3:1, 3, 5, 7, 9).

a. What specific benefits will you likely receive if you diligently keep God's commandments (Proverbs 3:1–2)?

_____

_____

b. What do you think it means to bind **mercy and truth** (NIV: "love and faithfulness") around your neck (Proverbs 3:3)?

_____

_____

_____

Balance Rule:

To learn how to balance the group discussion, go to www.Lamplighters USA.org/training.

ADDITIONAL
INSIGHTS

c. In what ways do you think these two qualities contribute to favor with God and man?

_____

_____

_____

_____

3. Prior to the fall of man (Genesis 3:1–6), Adam lived in perfect harmony with God (Genesis 1:31; 2:19, 25). Man's desire was to please and obey God. Adam was perfect (made without defect), but he was neither perfected nor confirmed in righteousness. Adam's failure in the garden moved him away from God and into complicity with Satan. Since the fall, man does not naturally obey God. In man's natural state (prior to salvation), he hides from God and values his own thoughts and ways above God's. In his natural state man is a child of God's wrath who will ultimately reap the eternal consequences of his estrangement from God if he is not saved (Ephesians 2:3; Hebrews 9:27).

a. Some Christians unwittingly claim God's promises without realizing that there may be one or more conditions that must be met before the promise is realized. List the three prerequisites (Proverbs 3:5–6a) that must be met *before* God's promise of divine guidance can be claimed in Proverbs 3:6b.

1. _____

_____ (v.____).

2. _____

_____ (v.____).

3. _____

_____ (v.____).

b. Do you think the phrases **trust in the Lord with all your heart** and **lean not on your own understanding** are basically synonymous (Proverbs 3:5)?
    If not, what is the distinction between the two?

_____

_____

_____

_____

4. Is there anything in your life (sinful habits, thoughts, or attitudes that you know are disobedient to God's Word) that proves that you are not trusting the Lord with all your heart—things that are preventing you from experiencing His joy and peace and the confidence that He is guiding you?
    If there is, what do you think you should do to stop leaning on your own understanding and to honor the Lord?

_____

_____

_____

5. Humility and virtuous living (Proverbs 3:7) bring healing and refreshment to our lives and indicate that we desire to live in harmony with God and His will (Proverbs 4:20–22). The Lord also commands us to **honor the Lord with your possessions, and with the firstfruits of all your increase** (Proverbs 3:9). List two truths this verse teaches about giving to the Lord.

1. _____

_____ (v.____).

2. _____

_____ (v.____).

6. Believers should willingly submit to another aspect of spiritual development (Proverbs 3:11–12). Name at least four benefits a believer receives when he responds correctly to the discipline of the Lord (Proverbs 3:12; Psalm 119:67, 71; Hebrews 12:7–12).

1. _____

_____ (v.____).

2. _____

_____ (v.____).

3. _____

_____ (v.____).

4. _____

_____ (v.____).

7. Wisdom is more profitable than silver, yields a better return than gold, and is more precious than rubies (Proverbs 3:13–15). No investment you will ever make can compare to gaining wisdom (Proverbs 3:15). What spiritual dividends or ROI (return-on-investment) can you expect to receive if you truly embrace God's wisdom (Proverbs 3:17–18)?

1. _____

_____ (v.____).

2. _____

_____ (v.____).

3. _____

_____ (v.____).

4. _____

_____ (v.____).

8. Wisdom is nothing new. It's not a social fad or the latest cliché—one destined to be overused and eventually discarded like a stained piece of clothing. What does the writer of Proverbs say about how wisdom was used in the past to convince his readers to make the adoption their passion and pursuit (Proverbs 3:19–20)?

_____

_____

_____

9. The writer of Proverbs continues to exhort the son to not lose sight of wisdom and discretion (Proverbs 3:21). List at least four additional benefits we will receive if we gain wisdom (Proverbs 3:22–26).

1. _____

    _____ (v._____).

2. _____

    _____ (v._____).

3. _____

    _____ (v._____).

4. _____

    _____ (v._____).

10. The relationship between truly submitting to God and man's virtuous living is inescapable. Moral conduct and ethical behavior within the Christian community, however, barely distinguish it from the world at large. When this happens, we dishonor God and mar the testimony of the church, and precious opportunities for reaching the lost slip away. From the following verses, restate the moral requirements that God expects from those who claim to be His true followers.

Proverbs 3:27–28. _____

Proverbs 3:29–30 _____

ADDITIONAL INSIGHTS

FIVE

WISDOM LEADS TO RIGHT LIVING

Read Proverbs 4; other references as given.

In the previous lesson you learned that there is a close relationship between right thinking (the wisdom of God) and wise or skillful living. You have also learned that rather than leaning or relying on your own understanding, you should embrace God's wisdom and let it guide all areas of your life (Proverbs 3:5–6).

In this lesson you will learn that the pursuit of wisdom must not be a weekend hobby, a casual sixty-minute Sunday investment in the eternal. Warren Wiersbe says, "Wisdom is not for the curious, but it is for the serious. There is a price to pay if you would gain wisdom, but there is a greater price to pay if you don't. The most expensive thing in the world is sin."

Now ask God to reveal Himself to you through His Word and transform you into the image of Jesus Christ.

No-Trespassing Rule:

To keep the Bible study on track, avoid talking about political parties, church denominations, and Bible translations.

ADD GROUP INSIGHTS BELOW

1. The change from **son** (Proverbs 3:1) to **children** (Proverbs 4:1) possibly indicating that the teaching in Proverbs 4:1–9 is more traditional in nature. Nevertheless, Solomon relentlessly continues his pursuit of helping his son (and us) gain wisdom.

    a. Take a minute to survey the father's instruction to his son to this point in the book of Proverbs. What words come to your mind when you think about the father's continuing efforts to help his children adopt the wisdom of God?

_____

_____

_____

b. If you are a parent, how would you compare your efforts to educate your children about the wisdom of God to the father's (Solomon's) efforts?

_____

_____

_____

If you are a Christian single, do you have the same passion as the father to see those in your life embrace God's truth? _____

Why? _____

_____

_____

c. What did the apostle Paul say about his own efforts to see Jesus Christ formed in the lives of others (Galatians 4:19)?

_____

_____

_____

2. In Proverbs 3:19–20 the writer said God used wisdom in the original act of creation. The teaching application is obvious: If God used wisdom to create the world, establish the heavens, and bring about the flood during the days of Noah (**all the fountains of the great deep were broken up;** Genesis 7:11), how much more do we need wisdom?

a. In Proverbs 4:3–9 the writer uses another great argument to help us understand the importance of gaining wisdom. What is it?

_____

_____

_____

b. What words and phrases did the grandfather use to describe the wisdom of God (Proverbs 4:3–9)?

_____

_____

_____

If you use table tents or name tags, it will help visitors feel more comfortable and new members will be assimilated more easily into your group.

———

ADDITIONAL
INSIGHTS

3. In addition to the words and phrases used in this and other passages of Scripture, God's people use other terms to describe the truth and wisdom of God—divinely-inspired, inerrant, etc. Non-Christians, on the other hand, use words such as *obsolete*, *irrelevant*, *outdated*, *fictional*, *anecdotal*, *mythical*, etc., to describe God's Word.

a. Why don't or can't unsaved people (the natural man) understand God's Word, and why are they not able to comprehend its infinite value (1 Corinthians 2:14)?

_____

_____

_____

_____

b. What or who is preventing them from understanding the truth of God (2 Corinthians 4:4; Mark 4:13–19)?

_____

_____

_____

4. Gaining God's wisdom should be a passionate pursuit for all believers. If you put the pursuit of God and His wisdom before all earthly pursuits, He will honor your commitment and bless your life (Proverbs 4:6, 8–12).

a. What specific commitments have you made to gain God's wisdom?

_____

_____

_____

_____

b. Many believers have made a commitment to read and study God's Word every day to gain the wisdom of God. Have you made this commitment?
YES   NO   I never thought of doing that.

Why? _____

_____

Would you be willing to make a commitment to read God's Word every day now? If you need help with a Bible reading plan, talk with your pastor or contact Lamplighters.

5. Wisdom will guide you into the right paths of life (Proverbs 4:11) and keep you from the evil way (Proverbs 4:14). The writer of Proverbs instructs us to avoid the paths of the wicked altogether (Proverbs 4:14–15). The apostle Paul, however, said that we were to live **in the midst of a crooked and perverse generation, among whom you shine as lights in the world** (Philippians 2:15). How can a believer avoid the paths of the wicked but still fulfill the biblical responsibility to live within a wicked and perverse society (Romans 12:1–2)?

_____

_____

_____

_____

_____

Use the side margins to write down spiritual insights from other people in your group. Add the person's name and the date to help you remember in the future.

_____

ADDITIONAL INSIGHTS

6. The wicked are so bent on doing evil that they cannot allow a day to pass without planning and executing their evil plans (Proverbs 4:16). What will they ultimately receive for the diligent planning and execution of wickedness (Proverbs 4:17, 19)?

_____

_____

_____

7. While the wicked stumble in the darkness of their own deception, the path of the righteous becomes brighter and brighter (Proverbs 4:18). Do you think **the perfect day** (Proverbs 4:18b; NIV: "the full light of day") refers to the time when we are in heaven, or does the phrase simply refer to the time when the sun has fully risen?

_____

Why? _____

_____

8. The father has repeatedly taught his son and other children to pursue wisdom. What additional things did the father tell his son to do to help him live wisely (Proverbs 4:20–27)?

1. _____

_____ (v._____).

2. _____

_____ (v._____).

3. _____

_____ (v._____).

4. _____

_____ (v._____).

5. _____

_____ (v._____).

9. Take a minute to reflect upon the father's teaching in Proverbs 1:2–4:19. What three key words would you use to describe his instruction to his son?

_____

_____

_____

10. a. What do you think it means to **keep your heart with all diligence** (Proverbs 4:23; NIV: "guard your heart")?

_____

_____

_____

_____

b. If you are a Christian, what are you doing to keep your heart with all diligence or guarding your heart?

_____

_____

_____

_____

_____

SIX

FOLLY HAS A FACE

Read Proverbs 5;
other references as given.

In the previous lesson you learned that a Christian must be diligent if he expects to gain God's wisdom. You also learned that Christians should not withdraw from the world (monasticism), but they should live wisely and shine as lights for God in a sinful world. Lastly, you learned that you need to guard your heart and mind with all diligence because your thinking will direct your life.

In this lesson Solomon moves from talking about the value of wisdom to warning his son and teaching how to identify the poster child of folly—the immoral woman or man. The father instructs his son how to recognize immoral people and the devastating consequences he'll face if he is caught in the web of her (or his) sin.

Before you begin, ask God to reveal Himself to you through His Word and transform you into the image of Jesus Christ.

1. The **immoral woman** (Hebrew *zarah*, sometimes translated "stranger," "strange woman," or "harlot") was estranged from the Israelite community because of her immoral behavior and her willful violation of God's law. There is a big difference between the kind of speech the father wants for his son and the speech of the immoral woman. What are some of the key differences (Proverbs 4:20–22, 24; 5:3–5)?

_____

_____

Transformation
Rule:

Seek for personal transformation, not mere information, from God's Word.

ADD GROUP
INSIGHTS BELOW

51

2. Proverbs 5–7 present the most complete profile of an immoral person (and his or her deceptive allurement) in the entire Bible. Business leaders, politicians, athletes, entertainers, and many others have fallen prey to the enticement of immoral people, and their lives and careers have been destroyed. Describe in your own words the true character of this instrument of destruction (Proverbs 5:4–6, 8–9, 20).

3. The Bible commands God's people to be morally pure. Believers should abstain from all forms of illicit sexual behavior. What does the apostle Paul tell the Thessalonians about the need for sexual purity (1 Thessalonians 4:3–8)?

4. Throughout church history, the church has believed that homosexuality is a sin rather than an alternative lifestyle. However, in recent years some liberal church denominations and even some Christians are questioning this position. What does the Bible teach about homosexuality (Romans 1:26–28, 1 Corinthians 6:9–11)?

Would you like to learn how to prepare a life-changing Bible study using a simple 4-step process? Contact Lamplighters and ask about ST-A-R-T.

ADDITIONAL
INSIGHTS

5. a. What will an immoral person receive for his or her indulgence (Proverbs 5:4–5, 10–14)?

_____

_____

_____

_____

   b. Immoral conduct can lead to destruction of our flesh (Proverbs 5:11). List some of the consequences, including health-related issues, that immoral people experience for dishonoring God in this area of their lives.

_____

_____

_____

_____

6. a. Name three individuals whose lives and witness for God were marred by immoral behavior (Genesis 49:3–4; 2 Samuel 11:1–4; 13:10–15).

   1. _____

       _____ (_____).

   2. _____

       _____ (_____).

   3. _____

       _____ (_____).

53

   b. The father gives two important pieces of advice to his son regarding association with the immoral woman (Proverbs 5:8; 6:25). What are they?

   _____

   _____

7. The Bible teaches a very important principle about moral purity in the Song of Solomon (Song of Solomon 2:7; 3:5; 5:8; 8:4). This moral principle will help you avoid sexual immorality. Restate this important biblical truth in your own words.

   _____

   _____

   _____

   _____

8. What do you think is the difference between love and lust?

   _____

   _____

   _____

9. In 1 Corinthians 13:4–7 the Bible lists the fifteen characteristics of biblical love. Of the fifteen characteristics, eight of them are in the negative (**love does not ...**), and seven characteristics are stated in the positive.

   a. List the eight "negative" (**love does not ...**) commands.

      1. _____

      2. _____

      3. _____

      4. _____

      5. _____

6. _____

7. _____

8. _____

b. List the seven positive characteristics of love (1 Corinthians 13:4–7).

1. _____

2. _____

3. _____

4. _____

5. _____

6. _____

7. _____

If the leader places a watch on the table, participants will feel confident that the Bible study will be completed on time. If the leader doesn't complete the lesson each week, participants will be less likely to do their weekly lessons, and the discussion will not be as rich.

_____

ADDITIONAL INSIGHTS

c. Now circle all those that you would like God to help you refrain from (Part a) and those you would like to do better (Part b).

10. a. In many parts of the world access to drinkable water is a matter of life and death. What or who do you think is referred to by the cistern (Proverbs 5:15)?

_____

b. What important truths about moral conduct are conveyed by this figure of speech (the cistern, Proverbs 5:15)?

_____

_____

_____

_____

11. The immoral person acquires bitterness of soul, disgrace, and perhaps even physical affliction if he violates God's

moral law (Proverbs 5:4, 11; 6:33). What words are used to describe the person who commits himself to moral purity within the marriage bond (Proverbs 5:18–19)?

_____

_____

_____

12. The young man is encouraged to be **enraptured** with the wife rather than with a strange woman (Proverbs 5:19–20). The Hebrew word (*sagah*) can mean "intoxicated" or "a staggering gait." In this context, it refers to the sexual infatuation an individual should have for his or her marriage partner.

   a. What important truth do these two verses teach us about sexual satisfaction within marriage (Proverbs 5:18–19)?

   _____

   _____

   _____

   b. Why should you abstain from all forms of immorality (Proverbs 5:21–23)?

      1. _____

         _____ (v._____).

      2. _____

         _____ (v._____).

      3. _____

         _____ (v._____).

SEVEN

ESCAPING ENTRAPMENT

Read Proverbs 6; other references as given.

In the previous chapter you learned the importance of avoiding immoral people and what the Bible teaches about sexual purity. You also learned the difference between love and lust and the fifteen characteristics of love.

In this lesson Solomon warns us about other forms of entrapment; 1) financial entrapment (Proverbs 6:1–5), 2) personal sin (Proverbs 6:6–11, 16–19), 3) slick schemers (Proverbs 6:12–15), and 4) adultery (Proverbs 6:20–35).

Now ask God to reveal Himself to you through His Word and transform you into the image of Jesus Christ.

If the leader asks all the study questions, the group discussion will be more likely to stay on track.

ADD GROUP INSIGHTS BELOW

1. The father warns his son about placing too much confidence in shallow promises of financial gain made by strangers (Proverbs 6:1–5; Hebrew *re*ª *...zar*: "neighbor, stranger"). The type of immature and misguided faith that focuses solely on the promise of financial gain, but doesn't evaluate the potential risks of an investment, often leads to financial entrapment and hinders a person's future usefulness for God.

    a. What advice does the father give his son if he finds himself lured into a foolish financial pledge (Proverbs 6:1–5)?

    _____

_____

_____

_____

b. The father uses two vivid illustrations to help his son see both why and how he can escape from this trap. What do you think he meant to teach his son by way of the gazelle and the bird (Proverbs 6:5)?

1. _____

_____

2. _____

_____

2. When a society becomes litigious (dominated by lawsuits and other legal actions), focus can dangerously shift from what is right and wrong to what is legal and illegal. If Christians fail to discern this subtle error, they can find themselves rationalizing sin and focusing more on whether an action is legal or illegal rather than on what God's Word says. What does God say about the words that we speak and our responsibility to others for them (Proverbs 6:1–5; Matthew 5:33–37)?

_____

_____

_____

_____

3. How can believers keep from becoming entrapped by making personal commitments concerning the future, when things may change that are beyond their control (James 4:13–17)?

_____

_____

4. It is likely that the father intended to warn his son against the individual who offered a promise of quick financial gain in exchange for a pledge to secure a loan. The Hebrew word (*re*ᵃ *...zar*) for **stranger** (Proverbs 6:1; NIV "neighbor") is likely a person whose only affiliation to the son is the promise of mutual financial benefit. Rather than looking for quick financial gain, the father instructed his son to consider the ant as an example of diligent labor that is rewarded (Proverbs 6:6–11). List two things all lazy and indolent people can learn from the ant (Proverbs 6:6–8).

The Bible says, *So then faith comes by hearing and hearing by the word of God* (Romans 10:17). Every time you humbly study God's Word, your faith grows.

ADDITIONAL INSIGHTS

1. _____

_____

2. _____

_____

5. Many Christians have a misguided concept of work. Rather than working hard and being good witnesses for Christ in the workplace, they view work as a curse and expect God to bless their poor work ethic. What does the Bible say about a person who is a lazy or a sluggard (Proverbs 6:9–11)?

_____

_____

6. Wicked people look to take advantage of others. They routinely use deceptive body language to "cover their tracks" so they cannot be caught when their deceit is exposed.

a. What kinds of sign language do these people use to deceive others (Proverbs 6:12–14)?

_____

_____

b. God is watching them as they scheme to deceive others. What will they receive in the end for their wickedness (Proverbs 6:15)?

_____

_____

7. God hates the works of darkness, and He hates the sinful attitudes that are behind them (Proverbs 6:16–19). The phrase (**six things the Lord hates, yes seven**, Proverbs 6:16) is a Hebrew figure of speech that is known as a numerical ladder. It shows that the list is not exhaustive. There are other things that the Lord hates and are an abomination to Him that are not included in this list (Leviticus 18:22; Deuteronomy 23:18; Proverbs 8:7; 11:1).

    a. List seven things that God hates and are an abomination to Him (Proverbs 6:16–19).

       1. _____

           _____ (v._____).

       2. _____

           _____ (v._____).

       3. _____

           _____ (v._____).

       4. _____

           _____ (v._____).

       5. _____

           _____ (v._____).

       6. _____

           _____ (v._____).

       7. _____

           _____ (v._____).

    b. Of these seven things, which ones have you engaged in during the past thirty days? Circle your answers.

God promises complete forgiveness for those who repent of their sin (1 John 1:9). If you committed any of these sins within the past month, would you be willing to repent right now and accept His full forgiveness?

It's a good time to begin praying and inviting new people for your next Open House.

ADDITIONAL
INSIGHTS

8. The father returns to a familiar source of entrapment—the immoral woman (Proverbs 6:20–35). This time, however, the immoral woman is further identified as an adulteress (a married woman [or man] who engages in sex outside marriage; Proverbs 6:26, 32, 34–35). The son is exhorted to listen to his father's and mother's warnings and to be on guard against entrapment at all times (**When you roam, when you sleep, when you awake**, Proverbs 6:20–22). What words are used to describe the woman who violates the marriage covenant she made to her husband before God (Proverbs 6:24–26)?

_____   _____

_____   _____

9. Many people, including celebrities, flaunt their immoral behavior by talking and even joking about "starter marriages," a "significant other" (a live-in lover), and "serial divorce" as if nothing is wrong or sinful about their conduct. Many Christians have abandoned God's standard of moral conduct and have adopted a worldly view of morality. When a society becomes confused about what is morally right, Christians must realize that His Word is true and His standard for moral behavior doesn't change, even if society falls farther and farther into an immoral abyss.

    a. What do the following verses teach about God's standard for moral behavior?

        i.   1 Corinthians 6:18–20: _____

        _____

ADDITIONAL
INSIGHTS

_____

_____

ii. Hebrews 13:4: _____

_____

_____

_____

b. What will the individual (Christian or non-Christian) receive for his folly if he violates God's moral standard by becoming sexually involved with a married woman (Proverbs 6:26–29, 31–35)?

_____

_____

_____

_____

_____

10. Now evaluate your view of moral behavior and compare it to God's standard of moral purity. If you are a Christian, in what areas of your life (actions, thoughts, speech, etc.) do you see yourself adopting the world's standard of moral conduct?

_____

_____

_____

_____

_____

If you are not sure if you are a Christian, turn to the back of this study guide, and read the Final Exam. It will explain how to trust Jesus Christ alone for eternal life.

EIGHT

HIGHWAY TO HELL

**Read Proverbs 7;
other references as given.**

In the previous lesson you learned that God's Word, not the changing norms of a fallen society, is the standard for moral conduct for believers. You also learned that all people, believers and nonbelievers alike, will reap the painful consequences of immoral misconduct.

In this lesson Solomon continues to warn his son (and us) about the seductive and destructive influence of immoral people. Using powerfully graphic language, he pleads with his son to avoid their path, which leads to death. In Proverbs 1, Solomon introduced us to the naïve or simple fool and said their hatred for wisdom will be their ruin. In Proverbs 7, he illustrates how the simple fool is entrapped and the price he pays for his folly.

Now ask God to reveal Himself to you through His Word and transform you into the image of Jesus Christ.

Is your study going well? Consider starting a new group. To learn how, go to www. Lamplighters USA.org/training.

ADD GROUP
INSIGHTS BELOW

1. Believers are encouraged to gain the wisdom of God *before* they face the trials of life. Theologian Larry Pettegrew said "Don't throw away truth just because you don't think you need it today. It is like money in the bank. You will need it sooner or later." What words or phrases are used to describe the level of intimacy God's people ought to have with wisdom before they actually employ it in real-life situations (Proverbs 7:1–4)?

_____

_____

_____

_____

2. The father's relentless appeal for his son to gain wisdom is not some spiritual exercise to fill the listless hours of adolescence. Wisdom offers intensely practical benefits to those who embrace it. Countless numbers of men and women who have rejected God's wisdom have had their lives destroyed by a lapse in moral judgment. Solomon warns his son (and us) not to be one of them.

a. In Proverbs 7:6–27 the father offers a graphic illustration of how his son can be trapped by an immoral woman. List the four individuals or groups of people who are mentioned in this illustration (Proverbs 7:6–10).

1. _____

_____ (v._____).

2. _____

_____ (v._____).

3. _____

_____ (v._____).

4. _____

_____ (v._____).

b. If you were asked to present a modern circumstance or setting where sexual entrapment might occur, what pictures or venues come to mind?

_____

_____

_____

_____

3. a. List three things about the young man's thinking and actions that made him an easy target for the immoral woman (Proverbs 7:7–9).

1. _____
   _____ (v._____).

2. _____
   _____ (v._____).

3. _____
   _____ (v._____).

It's time to choose your next study. Turn to the back of the study guide for a list of available studies or go online for the latest studies.

ADDITIONAL INSIGHTS

b. Name at least five characteristics of the immoral woman (or man) that will help you identify her and protect you from being trapped (Proverbs 6:24–25; 7:10–15; 9:13–18).

1. _____
   _____ (v._____).

2. _____
   _____ (v._____).

3. _____
   _____ (v._____).

4. _____
   _____ (v._____).

5. _____
   _____ (v._____).

4. Gone are the days when a man had to visit a squalid adult bookstore to purchase a sleazy magazine or X-rated video. The internet allows men and women to enter the dark world of immoral behavior in their homes, workplaces, schools, and even on their cell phones and tablets. Every day adult internet sites receive thousands of hits by people—all with the same ultimate end: broken lives and marriages, shattered

innocence, guilt, shame, and destroyed families.

    a. Have you intentionally viewed sexually explicit materials in any form in the past month?

_____

_____

    b. What recommendation would you give someone who was having trouble with pornography?

_____

_____

_____

_____

_____

5. The seductress is dressed like a harlot, and she aggressively pursues her prey (Proverbs 7:10, 13). She informs the young man that she has paid her peace offerings (Proverbs 7:14), a reference to the meat left over from the votive offering that she made at the sanctuary (Leviticus 7:11–21). It appears that she was informing the young man that she had something for him to eat and that she was ceremonially clean, perhaps cleansed from her menstrual cycle (a bold statement of her sexual availability).

    a. She propositions the young man with promises of unbridled love (Proverbs 7:16–18), but it's obvious that she doesn't know the difference between love and lust. Describe in one sentence the difference between love and lust by completing the following sentence:

Lust _____

_____ ,

but love _____

_____ .

b. Evaluate the way you love others, especially those closest to you. How could you love them more?

_____

_____

_____

_____

6. The adulteress assures the young man that they will not be caught because her husband will be gone for a long time (Proverbs 7:19–20). With **enticing speech** (literally, "the greatness of her words") she causes him to yield. He goes, not knowing that he follows her **as an ox goes to the slaughter** (Proverbs 7:22).

a. What additional words and phrases are used to help the young man understand the devastation that lies ahead (Proverbs 7:22–27)?

_____

_____

_____

_____

b. What words or comments have you heard people say (in person, movies, television, internet, etc.) to entrap others into immoral behavior?

_____

_____

_____

_____

7. The solicitation of young men (and women) to engage in immoral behavior is not limited to clandestine meetings between consenting adults in darkened alleys. The average young person is bombarded by an endless river of moral

sewage that flows from television, movies, videos, books, magazines, and the internet. School-aged children are exposed to sex education programs in the public schools that encourage them to "wait until they are ready" rather than promoting God's standard of sexual abstinence until marriage. Some public schools even provide a list of counseling resources for students who are questioning their sexual identity. What do you think individual Christians and churches can do to protect young people more effectively?

_____

_____

_____

_____

8. In Proverbs 1:8–33 the father identified the two voices who are calling out to his son—the voice of folly and the voice of wisdom. The father (the voice of wisdom) warns the son not to listen to the seductress (the voice of folly). Her house (her life, her ways) is the highway to hell, **descending to the chambers of death** (Proverbs 7:27).

a. With all this warning, including the graphic depiction of the consequences of immoral behavior, why do you think many Christians still engage in sexual sin?

_____

_____

_____

b. What have you learned from this passage of Scripture that will change your life from this point forward?

_____

_____

_____

Nine

In Wisdom's Own Words

**Read Proverbs 8;
other references as given.**

In the first seven chapters of Proverbs, Solomon exhorts his son (and us) to embrace wisdom—not just as a principle of life, but personally as a cherished life companion. Solomon personalized folly, describing it as an immoral woman who is seeking to destroy his son's life. But folly is not just an immoral woman; folly is anyone who lives in rebellion to God and His moral laws and invites others to join in sin.

In Proverbs 8 there is a significant change in the narrative. In the first seven chapters the father was appealing to His son, but in Proverbs 8 wisdom herself appeals to all who will listen. What wisdom says in this chapter should encourage you to pursue her with all your heart.

Now ask God to reveal Himself to you through His Word and transform you into the image of Jesus Christ.

Many groups study the Final Exam the week after the final lesson for three reasons: (1) someone might come to Christ, (2) believers gain assurance of salvation, (3) group members learn how to share the gospel.

———

ADD GROUP
INSIGHTS BELOW

1. Throughout the first nine chapters of Proverbs, wisdom and folly are personified and contrasted by two women. Folly is a crafty seductress who promises pleasure but delivers pain and death. She is secretive, devious, and manipulative, and those who follow her ways become her victims. Folly works in the darkness and preys upon the simple and naïve. To whom does wisdom call, and where is her voice heard (Proverbs 1:20–21; 8:1–5)?

_____

2. a. It is often difficult for Christians to know exactly where to find wisdom. Some say to let your conscience be your guide, while others say to let your heart guide you (subjective experience). Still others say to find an "anointed" spiritual leader to follow. Where should a Christian look to find God's wisdom (John 17:17)?

    b. How can a Christian gain more wisdom (John 14:21)?

3. Wisdom calls to all men, but she makes a special appeal to the simple (to gain prudence) and to fools (to gain understanding; Proverbs 8:5). Wisdom attempts to motivate her listeners by declaring that she has worthy things to offer them. What words or phrases are used to describe the things that wisdom will give you if you seek her with all your heart (Proverbs 8:6–11)?

4. The words of wisdom (*wisdom, truths, principles*, etc.) are not hard to understand to those who embrace them (**They are all plain to him who understands, and right to those who find knowledge**; Proverbs 8:9). It is not a matter of

understanding that prevents people from accepting the truth; it is a matter of the will. Author Mark Twain said, "It is not what I don't understand about the Bible that bothers me, it is what I do understand that bothers me."

a. If wisdom is found through knowing and obeying God's Word, what commitments do you think a believer should make to God about his submission to the Word of God?

_____

_____

_____

_____

b. If wisdom and truth come from God's Word, what commitments do you think a church should make to help the congregants gain wisdom?

_____

_____

_____

_____

5. The value of wisdom is not just for the simple and naïve - it is also for those in positions of power and authority (Proverbs 8:4, 16). Wisdom resides together with prudence (Heb. *ormah*), meaning it provides the individual who possesses it with right knowledge for special circumstances. For example, those in positions of power need wisdom so they can provide good counsel to others and avoid the temptation to become prideful of their position and achievements.

a. In addition to those mentioned in Proverbs 8:15–16, in what areas do you think all leaders (fathers, mothers, employers, pastors, etc.) need to exercise wisdom?

_____

_____

Having trouble with your group? A Lamplighters trainer can help you solve the problem.

ADDITIONAL INSIGHTS

_____

_____

b. In what areas of your life do you need more wisdom right now?

_____

_____

_____

6. To many people, wisdom often seems elusive. They might live according to God's wisdom in some areas of their lives, but they rely on our own understanding in other areas.

a. What does God promise to those who love and seek diligently God and His wisdom (Proverbs 8:17; Matthew 7:7–8; James 1:5)?

_____

_____

_____

_____

_____

_____

b. What else does God promise those who diligently seek wisdom (Proverbs 8:18–21)?

_____

_____

_____

_____

_____

_____

7. In Proverbs 8:22–31 wisdom is pictured as the master craftsman who assisted God during the time of creation. When God finished the creation of this world, He said that it was very good (Genesis 1:31). Many people talk about Mother Nature or Mother Earth, which robs God of the glory due His name in creation. Many schools and communities celebrate Earth Day, but they forget the One who created the earth. On the other hand, many people, including some Christians, abuse God's creation and treat it like their personal garbage dump. What perspective do you think a Christian should have toward the earth (Genesis 1:28; Psalm 24:1)?

    _____

    _____

    _____

It's time to order your next study. Turn to the back of the study guide for a list of available studies or go online at www. LamplightersUSA. org for the latest studies.

ADDITIONAL INSIGHTS

8. Perhaps the son and other children were saying, *"We get the point. You want us to get wisdom."* But knowing about wisdom is much different than possessing it. Wisdom goes beyond mere knowledge. It has an action component to it. Wisdom is God-given knowledge humbly put to work.

    a. In Matthew 7:24–27 Jesus taught a parable about two men. One built his house on the sand, and the other built his on the rock. What truth was Jesus attempting to teach in this parable (Matthew 7:24–27)?

        _____

        _____

        _____

        _____

        _____

    b. When was the folly of the man who built his life on the sand revealed (Matthew 7:24–27)?

        _____

c. How does this parable apply to you?

_____

_____

9. The believers to whom the book of Hebrews was addressed were encouraged not to follow the example of their forefathers who were delivered from Egypt. During the time of the Exodus the Israelites were given the Law of God and the promise of entering a land flowing with milk and honey. Why did the ancient Israelites perish in the wilderness even though they had been given the Law of God and His promises (Hebrews 4:1–2)?

_____

_____

10. Take a close look at your life before God. In which areas of your life do you see an unwillingness to yield yourself completely to God and His wisdom?

a. Relationships (marriage, sexual purity).
b. Worship (fellowship with other believers in a Bible-preaching church, personal study and prayer).
c. Financial stewardship (giving to the Lord and helping those in need).
d. Priorities (God, family, work, leisure).
e. Forgiveness (unforgiveness, anger, resentment, slander).

10. If you identified any areas above where you need to yield yourself more to God, what would prevent you from surrendering to God right now?

_____

_____

_____

_____

TEN

WISDOM'S REWARDS

Read Proverbs 9;
other references as given.

In the previous lesson wisdom made her appeal directly to her listeners. She informed them of the benefits of embracing her and promised to give them good counsel, sound judgment, understanding, and strength (Proverbs 8:14). Everyone who seeks wisdom will find her (Proverbs 8:17). Lastly, she said riches, honor, enduring wealth, and prosperity are hers to give (Proverbs 8:18).

In this lesson wisdom makes one last appeal before the two-line proverbs begin in chapter 10. In Proverbs 9, Solomon returns to some of the original themes of chapter 1 (the foolish woman, the foolish young man, the fear of the Lord).

Now ask God to reveal Himself to you through His Word and transform you into the image of Jesus Christ.

Final Exam:

Are you meeting next week to study the Final Exam? To learn how to present it effectively, contact Lamplighters.

———

ADD GROUP
INSIGHTS BELOW

1. In Proverbs 8, wisdom is pictured as a wise master builder who worked with God to create the world. Now wisdom constructs her own home, prepares a lavish feast, and sends her maidens out to invite the guests (Proverbs 9:2–3).

   a. Whom does she invite to her feast (Proverbs 9:3–4)?

   _____

   _____

   b. What does wisdom offer to serve her guests (Proverbs

75

9:5; the obvious answer is bread and wine according to the metaphor, but try to give a more complete answer from the passage)?

_____

_____

2. One of the invited guests, the scoffer, does not accept wisdom's invitation (Proverbs 9:7–8) The scoffer is a fool who not only hates wise instruction, but also hates those who attempt to impart wisdom (Proverbs 9:7, 9).

   a. How will a scoffer respond if you attempt to instruct him (Proverbs 9:7– 8a; 13:1; 15:12; 21:24)?

_____

_____

_____

_____

   b. How does a wise man respond to another person's attempts to instruct him (Proverbs 9:8–9)?

_____

_____

   c. Take a minute to evaluate how you respond to correction at work, … at home, … and at church to the teaching and preaching of God's Word. Do you respond like a naïve fool who remains uncommitted to truth even when he hears it (Proverbs 1:22–26)? Do you respond like the wise man who is grateful to those who correct him and gains wisdom (Proverbs 9:9)? Do you respond like the scoffer who hates instruction and those who offer it (Proverbs 9:8)?

_____

_____

3. The main body of two-line proverbs begins in the next chapter, and a great deal of understanding can be gained if you learn to identify the various types of proverbs.

Would you like to learn how to lead someone through this same study? It's not hard. Go to www.Lamplighters USA.org to register for *free* online leadership training.

ADDITIONAL
INSIGHTS

   a. In Proverbs 9:7 there is an excellent example of one of the four different types of proverbs. What type of proverb is found in this verse (see Introduction, page 12 for the various types of proverbs)?

_____

   b. If you study the parallelism of the proverb found in Proverbs 9:7, you will gain a better understanding of the verse. List the word or phrase the writer uses for the word or phrase listed below.

     1. Correct:

     _____

     2. Scoffer (NIV "mocker"):

     _____

     3. Gets shame (NIV "invites insult"):

     _____

4. Why do you think unsaved people (those who are not born again, according to the Bible) do not accept God and His wisdom when it offers so many great benefits to them (John 3:19–20; 2 Corinthians 4:4)?

_____

_____

_____

_____

5. It is understandable that those who have never been born again reject the truth of God's Word. However, the Bible

teaches that many of God's people also reject the truth.

a. Why do some Christians reject the truth (2 Timothy 4:3–4)?

_____

_____

_____

_____

b. What was Timothy, who was serving as a pastor at the time, to do when the believers rejected the truth (2 Timothy 4:2, 5)?

_____

_____

_____

_____

6. Take a moment to examine your relationship with God in light of what you have learned in this Bible study. Do you have a hunger for God and His Word that is consistent with the scriptural prerequisites for gaining wisdom, or do you have "itching ears" and only accept those things that please you? Check the answer that reflects your present appetite for truth.

__ I have a burning passion to know God and His Word.

__ I have a desire for wisdom and for knowing God and His Word, but it is not as strong as it should be.

__ I don't have much of an appetite for wisdom and knowing God's Word. I can take it or leave it.

__ I haven't had much of a desire for knowing God and His Word, but I want to.

7. What could you do to gain a greater appetite to know God through His Word?

_____

_____

_____

For more discipleship help, sign up to receive the Disciple-Maker Tips—a bi-monthly email that provides insights to help your small group function more effectively.

ADDITIONAL INSIGHTS

8. The first thing a Christian must do to acquire the wisdom of God is to understand **the fear of the Lord** (Proverbs 9:10; note: It is **the beginning of wisdom**). Although the phrase **the fear of the Lord** appears frequently in Scripture, many believers do not know what it means. Even the prophet Jonah appeared to be confused when he said he feared the Lord even though he was running from God' presence (Jonah 1:4–9).

   a. To gain wisdom, you must gain a thorough understanding of the meaning of this phrase. The following verses have been carefully chosen to help you develop an accurate definition of this important phrase (Deuteronomy 10:12; Job 28:28; Psalm 33:8; Proverbs 14:26). What do you think is the meaning of the phrase the **fear of the Lord**?

   _____

   _____

   _____

   _____

   b. Most people are afraid of something (failure, physical pain, disease, rejection, poverty, success, death, being alone, etc.). Unless fear is yielded to God, it can control you and keep you from loving and knowing God. What is your greatest fear, and how does Satan use it to keep you from trusting and obeying the Lord?

   _____

   _____

_____

_____

c. The Bible says that God has not given us a spirit of fear (2 Timothy 1:7). Where then do you think all fear (except the fear of the Lord) comes from, and what is its cure (Isaiah 41:10, 13; 43:1)?

_____

_____

_____

_____

9. As you conclude this study of Proverbs chapters 1–9, reflect on what we have studied. What are the most important spiritual truths that you have learned in these first nine chapters of Proverbs?

1. _____

_____ (v.____).

2. _____

_____ (v.____).

3. _____

_____ (v.____).

10. If you had to pick only truth that you learned from this passage of Scripture—one that will change your life forever—what is that one truth?

_____

_____

_____

LEADER'S GUIDE

Lesson 1: Knowledge and Wisdom

1. a. Answers will vary. Answers could include the following: Wisdom is knowing what to do and when to do it.
   b. Answers will vary. Answers could include the following: Knowledge is knowing; knowledge is understanding facts about a particular subject or topic. Knowledge is the theoretical, intuitive, or practical understanding of something. Other answers could apply.
   c. Answers will vary, but they should include something like the following: Wisdom is God-given knowledge humbly put to work. Wisdom surpasses knowledge. Wisdom includes the ability to rightly apply knowledge in the proper situation and at the appropriate time.

2. a. Answers will vary.
   b. 1. An individual must believe that God will give wisdom to all men and pray for its appropriation (James 1:5–6).
      2. An individual must exercise wisdom in daily life (James 3:13).
      3. An individual must allow the Holy Scriptures to define who he is (a sinner), convict him that he cannot save himself, and convince him of his need for salvation in Jesus Christ (2 Timothy 3:15)

3. 1. Personal conduct
   2. Interpersonal relations
   3. Work
   4. Money management
   5. Effective communications
   6. Emotional Health
   7. Business and personal ethics

4. A thorn in the hand of a drunkard.

5. The law, the prophets and the writings.

6. Jesus Christ.

7. 1. Proverbs gives us wisdom and understanding about God and His ways (Proverbs 1:2).
    2. Proverbs gives us discernment to help us know the difference between truth and folly (Proverbs 1:2).
    3. Proverbs provides instruction in wise behavior, righteous living, justice, and equity (Proverbs 1:3).
    4. Proverbs gives us prudence so we don't have to be naïve and we can make wise choices in life (Proverbs 1:4).
    5. Proverbs gives young people knowledge about life and discretion (Proverbs 1:4).
    6. Proverbs helps us understand the biblical proverbs and figures of speech, the sayings of the wise, and their riddles (Proverbs 1:6, perhaps this includes parables and other figures of speech).

8. a. The simple (Proverbs 1:4), the young (Proverbs 1:4), and the wise man (Proverbs 1:5).
    b. The naive or simple is open to any and every thought and danger because he is uncommitted to a biblical perspective of life. The youth has not learned to recognize the dangers of life, and his inexperience has made him vulnerable as well.

9. Answers will vary.

10. A Christian must gain a genuine fear of the Lord. This means that he must acknowledge God's authority over every aspect of his life. This begins with being born again, and it continues on in life as the individual pursues God and His wisdom. For a clear presentation of God's plan of salvation, see the Final Exam in the back of this Bible study guide manual.

11. a. Answers will vary.
    b. Answers will vary.

Lesson 2: Two Voices Are Calling

1. a. Both parents are responsible for helping their children develop skill in daily living (Proverbs 1:8, Deuteronomy 6:4–7). It appears, however, that the father is ultimately responsible because of his God-ordained leadership role within the family (Ephesians 6:1–4).

b. *Parent portion of the question:* Answers will vary but may include the following: Modeling a godly life before the children, consistent times of Bible instruction, active participation of the family in a Bible-believing church, spontaneous discussions about how biblical truth applies to the various aspects of daily living. Other answers could apply.
Unmarried portion of the question: The acceptance of this important responsibility of providing biblical instruction for the children should be a major consideration prior to marriage.

2. A graceful wreath or an ornament can impart beauty and enhance one's appearance. A son's or daughter's life is beautified or enhanced when they embrace wise parental instruction. The beautification is often reflected in a pleasantness of manner and other aspects of attractiveness that extend far beyond their physical attractiveness.

3. a. The solicitation to become involved in ungodly adventures is often directed toward those who are dangerously open-minded or naïve (the simple). The naive often reveal by their conduct and speech that they can be taken advantage of by those who are shrewd and deceitful. Because the naïve are not committed to following the path of wisdom, they often find themselves associating with the wrong people who have no regard for God and His ways.
   b. 1. They are violent (Proverbs 1:11, 16).
      2. They are aggressively solicitous (Proverbs 1:10, 11, 14).
      3. They have no respect for the property rights of others (Proverbs 1:13).
      4. They are self-deceived and oblivious to their own coming destruction (Proverbs 1:18–19).
      5. They are greedy (Proverbs 1:12–13).
   c. The innocent (Proverbs 1:11) and themselves (Proverbs 1:18).

4. a. Answers will vary but could include the following: sexual exploitation, including luring young people into prostitution; pornography; abortion; illicit drug use, distribution, and drug-related crimes; income tax evasion; Ponzi schemes; fraud; money-making schemes of televangelists. Other answers could apply.
   b. 1. The simple are promised social acceptance by the group (Proverbs 1:11, 14).

2. The simple are enticed by the opportunity for easy financial gain without apparent consequences (Proverbs 1:13).
3. The simple are promised to be in a position of power over others (**Let us swallow them alive**, Proverbs 1:12).
4. The simple are promised an equal share of the spoil (Proverbs 1:14). This last enticement would be particularly appealing to someone who is naïve.

5. 1. The father said not to go (Proverbs 1:10, 15).
   2. Innocent people will be hurt, and someone may even die because of their actions (Proverbs 1:11–12).
   3. The scheme that these sinners are planning is illegal (Proverbs 1:13).
   4. The actions of these rebels are sinful and evil (Proverbs 1:16).
   5. Those who participate in these evil deeds will eventually be caught, and their lives will be ruined (Proverbs   1:17–19).

6. a. Wisdom is readily available to anyone who will invest the time and effort to acquire it.
   b. Answers will vary but should look something like this: "How long will those of you who are uncommitted to God's ways and are dangerously open-minded continue to live according to your own faulty human reason?" Other answers could apply.
   c. Answers will vary.
   d. The believer should study Proverbs and other passages of Scripture to develop discernment. The believer should also resist the temptation to make quick decisions that he will regret later (Proverbs 28:20). He should also solicit the counsel of godly men and women regarding important decisions. Other answers could apply.

7. 1. God will not help them in their time of distress (Proverbs 1:24–26).
   2. God will not answer their prayers in the time of calamity even if they seek Him diligently in their hour of distress (Proverbs 1:28).
   3. God will allow them to reap the full extent of what they have sown (Proverbs 1:31; this means that they will be given no mercy by God at that time).
   4. They will eventually be destroyed for their lack of wisdom (Proverbs 1:32).
   5. They will continue to forfeit God's peace, which is available to all those who seek His wisdom (Proverbs 1:33).

8. a. God's offer of wisdom is available to all those who make the diligent pursuit of His wisdom a lifetime goal. This promise of James 1:5 does not apply to those who call upon God in the day of their calamity if they have not diligently sought wisdom prior to that time. The "but" (James 1:6) says the prayer for wisdom must also be accompanied by faith, which is not likely present in those who are merely looking to escape the consequences of their folly.

    b. Some allow Satan to steal the truth from their minds (Mark 4:15). Some allow the problems and trials of life to distract them from pursuing the truth (Mark 4:16–17). Some others are more concerned about gaining material things than pursuing God (Mark 4:19). They don't want their sins to be exposed (John 3:19). They cannot understand the truth because they are not true Christians (2 Corinthians 2:14). They are not willing to live by faith (Hebrews 4:2).

    c. Answers will vary.

Lesson 3: The Value of Wisdom

1. a. In the immediate context it includes the father's admonitions contained in Proverbs 1–9. In the broader context it includes the actual proverbs (Proverbs 10:1) and all the godly instruction the father would give his son throughout his lifetime.

    b. The father refers to the words and commandments of God as his words and commandments because he had appropriated God's wisdom into his own life. When an individual accepts the wisdom of God by faith, the truth becomes his intimate companion, protector, and friend. Wisdom becomes his own (**my commandments**) in the sense that it becomes part of his thinking, his actions, and his character. Wisdom was so intertwined with the father's being that he could rightfully say these were his words and commandments even though they originated with God.

2. The individual must understand that most teaching will not be used immediately. Wisdom is a treasure to be stored for the future when an opportunity occurs whereby the wise instruction will be of great benefit. In the interim, wisdom will help an individual develop beliefs that will produce attitudes and actions that will direct the course of his or her life.

3. While the various individual aspects must be employed in the pursuit of wisdom, it likely means that there must be a passionate pursuit of this noble prize that includes every aspect of man's being.

4. a. "If you ..." The use of the phrase introduces a series of contingencies or qualifying conditions that must be met before an individual can expect to realize the benefits listed in Proverbs 2:5. The inclusion of these conditions indicates that there is the possibility that a Christian may not be willing to exert the spiritual energy necessary to accomplish the task and reap the benefits.
   b. The repetition of the phrase "if you" highlights the importance and significance of the personal decisions each person must make if he or she expects to gain God's wisdom. All conditions must be met before the individual can possess the wisdom of God.

5. Answers will vary but could include something like the following: If you seek wisdom like you would seek a luxury car, a lake cabin, a coveted position at work, a special person you would like to marry, money, an academic degree, then ...

6. Most Christians need to be more diligent in their pursuit of God and His wisdom, but they shouldn't attempt to live for God in their own power (Galatians 3:1–5). They need to make definite spiritual commitments to pursue God and trust that He will give them the power to live for Him. God will reveal truth to them, and the truth will set them free from the corruption in this world. Too many believers are "waiting on God" when God has clearly instructed them to pursue Him, but always in the grace and strength of the Lord.

7. a. The word *then* makes the promises for wisdom, discernment, protection from error, etc., conditional.
   All the conditions stated in Proverbs 2:1–4 must be met before the benefits of Proverbs 2:5 can be claimed.
   b. The believer is promised: 1. Understanding of the fear of the Lord (Proverbs 2:5a). 2. Knowledge of God's plan for man on earth (Proverbs 2:5b). 3. Wisdom (Proverbs 2:6, 10). 4. Divine protection (Proverbs 2:7b–8). 5. A love for God's truth (Proverbs 2:10b), 6. Discretion (Proverbs 2:11), 7. Deliverance from evil people (Proverbs 2:12, 16).

c. Man's initial response to God's Word will not necessarily be thrill and excitement. He must pursue God and His Word by faith, knowing that God will honor his efforts and the truth will become pleasant to his soul.

8. Knowledge and understanding. Knowledge is a comprehension of God's truth for daily living. Understanding is the wisdom to apply God's principles for daily living in a consistently prudent manner.

9. a. Wicked men (Proverbs 2:12–15, **those who leave the paths of uprightness** ...) and immoral women (Proverbs 2:16).
    b. Ungodly people often speak perverse things—both their words and thoughts are contrary to God (Proverbs 2:12), and they often celebrate and rejoice over doing evil (Proverbs 2:14). Immoral people often use flattery and seductive speech to accomplish their sexual objectives (Proverbs 2:16)
    c. Answers will vary.
    d. Answers will vary.

10. Her husband and God (Proverbs 2:17b). It is interesting that the covenant she made with her husband was before God, even though nothing is mentioned about her relationship with God other than that she is immoral.

Lesson 4: Wisdom Will Guide You

1. a. Parents should not allow themselves to become discouraged if they find themselves repeating the same instructions to their children. The fallen nature of man, along with children's immature mental abilities, make the repetition of wisdom necessary. However, they should look for creative ways to impart truth to their children, realize the natural developmental stage of a child, and avoid harping or nagging on them.
    b. Children should realize that it is their parents' responsibility to instruct them until the truths are firmly ingrained into their lives. When parents repeat truths to their children, most often it is because the parents do not think they have fully grasped the truth.

2. a. A good, long life filled with peace (Proverbs 3:2).
    b. The believer should develop an intimate relationship with mercy and truth and allow them to be his constant companions. The believer

should not lose sight of them as he goes about the affairs of life.

c. If we are not truthful with God, we will forfeit fellowship with Him that will result in unanswered prayer, loss of peace, and many other negative things. If we are not honest with others, they will discover our deceitfulness before long and distrust us. If we are not merciful toward others, they will naturally pull back from us as a protective measure, which will hinder our ability to minister to them.

3. a. 1. The believer must trust the Lord fully. 2. The believer must not rely on his own reason when his thoughts are contrary to God and His Word. 3. The believer must acknowledge God's authority over all aspects of his life.

b. They are two sides of the same coin. If we are trusting God with all our hearts, then we are not leaning on our own understanding. The first phrase looks at the believer's responsibility toward God, and the second looks at the believer's responsibility toward himself. He is to trust God and not trust himself. Someone said, "Faith is letting God have the last word when our mind is arguing with His Word."

4. Answers will vary.

5. 1. God is honored when His people give back to Him.
   2. God expects His people to give back the first portion of their possessions.

6. 1. We are reassured of His love (Proverbs 3:12).
   2. We learn to obey the Word of God more fully (Psalms 119:67, 71).
   3. We are reminded that we are God's children (Hebrews 12:7–9).
   4. We become more godly or righteous in our daily living (Hebrews 12:10–12).

7. The believer gains peace and the tree of life, which is the symbol of vitality and fullness of life. The believer's life will also be blessed.

8. The Lord used wisdom to create the earth and the heavens. These verses show the wisdom was used from the foundation of this cosmos, and those who surrender to God's wisdom place themselves in harmony with the eternal plan of God, including creation.

9. 1. The son will have a beauty to his life and live in safety (Proverbs 3:22–23).
   2. The son will not stumble through life (Proverbs 3:23b).
   3. The son will not have to live in fear or worry about trouble or sudden tragedy (Proverbs 3:24–25).
   4. The son will sleep well (Proverbs 3:24).
   5. The son will have the confidence that the Lord will be his guide (Proverbs 3:26).

10. a. Christians should give to the needy according to their means and repay others without delay. They should not offer feeble excuses that are really lies to avoid their financial and other social debts.
    b. Christians should not devise evil against their neighbors. Perhaps the reference here is to groundless lawsuits against acquaintances and others. Another possibility could be phony legal actions against insurance companies for the sake of gaining a claim, which will be paid by the policyholders, including some of the person's neighbors.

Lesson 5: Wisdom Leads to Right Living

1. a. Answers will vary. The answer should include words such as *relentless, passionate, convicted, diligent, determined, committed, faithful,* and *responsible.* Other answers could apply.
   b. Answers will vary. / Answers will vary.
   c. Paul agonized like a woman in labor over the Galatian believers' spiritual development. The Greek word for "form" (*morphow*) means the essential form rather than mere outward shape. Paul was saying that he was willing, if possible, to experience labor-like contraction pains until genuine Christlike character was formed in the Galatian believers.

2. a. The wisdom the father desired to pass down to his son had been passed down from previous generations. The son's grandfather had taught the principles of wisdom to him (the father) when he was young. The point is this: wisdom has been a family treasure for generations. Perhaps the special bond that often exists between a grandparent and grandchild had a special appeal to the son.

b. **My words** and **my commands** (Proverbs 4:4), **understanding, words of my mouth** (Proverbs 4:5), **love her** (Proverbs 4:6), **the principal thing** (Proverbs 4:7), **exalt** and **honor** (Proverbs 4:8), **ornament of grace** and **crown of glory** (Proverbs 4:9).

3. a. Unsaved people don't possess the spiritual capacity to comprehend the things of God apart from the enlightening ministry of the Holy Spirit. Spiritual truth is foolishness to them, and they often ridicule it and the people who talk about God's truth because they cannot understand God's truth. At salvation, the natural man is born again and receives the Spirit of God, which enables him to begin to comprehend God and His Word. For a complete explanation about how to be born again according to the Bible, read the "Final Exam" section in the back of this study guide.

b. The god of this world (Satan) has blinded the minds of all the people in the world. This prevents them from understanding the truth. Only salvation through Jesus Christ can remove this spiritual blindness and reveal the truth to them.

4. a. Answers will vary.
   b. Answers will vary.

5. The believer must present himself to God as a living sacrifice. He must "take his stand with Jesus" and turn his back on the world's acceptance and its lusts. He must actively resist every attempt by Satan and the unsaved to force him to adopt the world's values, goals, and priorities. He should not allow himself to be conformed to this world. He must allow his mind to be renewed and transformed into the image of Jesus Christ. He should submit himself to the regular preaching of God's Word, fellowship, and confession of sin and engage in daily Bible study. He should seek to live a godly life in an ungodly world, where he is to shine a light in the darkness and seek to bring others to a saving knowledge of Jesus Christ. If believers remove themselves physically from a society (monasticism), they remove themselves from the people Jesus died for and wants to rescue from eternal judgment.

6. They reap what they have sown—wickedness and violence (Proverbs 4:17). They also experience confusion as a result of forsaking God's wisdom

and its promise of divine guidance (Proverbs 4:19). The law of "sowing and reaping" has three principles that every believer would be wise to remember: 1. We reap the same thing that we sow. 2. We reap later than we sow. 3. We usually reap more than we sow.

7. The time when the sun has fully risen. The second possible interpretation is an example of an "allegorical interpretation" or it is sometimes called spiritualizing a verse. This happens when the student assigns an incorrect "hidden" spiritual meaning to a verse. The verse should be understood at face value unless it is obvious that it is a metaphor. Allegorical interpretation usually leads to an incorrect interpretation of Scripture.

8. 1. The father told the son to make wisdom the focus of his life (Proverbs 4:21).
    2. He told his son to keep or guard his heart (mind, will, and emotions) with all diligence because his heart was the wellspring of life (Proverbs 4:23).
    3. He told his son to cleanse himself of all ungodly and perverse speech (Proverbs 4:24).
    4. He told his son to guard his eyes so that he would be careful to refrain from looking at things that would distract him (Proverbs 4:25).
    5. He told his son to be careful where he went and to keep away from evil (Proverbs 4:26–27).

9. Answers will vary but could include the following: *direct, specific, clear, concise, powerful, loving*. Other answers could apply.

10. a. A Christian must keep watch over his heart (mind) because it is the starting point of all decision-making. He should be diligent to guard and protect his thinking, as well as be careful whom he allows to influence him, because his thoughts will eventually lead to actions. Proverbs 23:7 says, **For as [a man] thinks in his heart** (mind)**, so is he.**
    b. Answers will vary.

Lesson 6: Folly Has a Face

1. The son is instructed to acquire wise words by developing an aptitude

for hearing them and recognizing their importance. He is also instructed to put away all forms of ungodly and perverse speech from his mind and mouth (Proverbs 4:20–22, 24). The immoral woman speaks words that are smoother than oil to the listener's ear, but they are deceitful. Her words eventually trap the listener and lead him to the grave (Proverbs 5:3–5). The father's words are wisdom; the immoral woman's words are a lie.

2. The immoral woman's speech is convincing, but it is also extremely dangerous (Proverbs 5:3–5). She is an agent of the devil and leads those who follow her to hell (Proverbs 5:5). Wise people stay far away from her because she traps her victims (Proverbs 5:8–9). She causes them to waste their lives and strength as they are enticed by her empty words and covet her lustful charms (Proverbs 5:9). She entraps her victims with her seductive beauty and promises them immoral sexual pleasure that does not have devastating consequences. This is a lie (Proverbs 5:20).

3. It is God's will for believers to abstain from all forms of sexual immorality (1 Thessalonians 4:3). Paul said they should learn how to control their sexual appetites in a manner that is holy and honorable (1 Thessalonians 4:3–4). He said there should be a clear distinction between the sexual conduct of the unsaved and the saved (1 Thessalonians 4:5). He said they should not take advantage of other people sexually because God will punish them for these sins (1 Thessalonians 4:6). He said that if the Thessalonian believers reject what he has written, they are rejecting God, not him (1 Thessalonians 4:8).

4. The Bible teaches that homosexuality is a sin. It is a by-product of not honoring God as God and not being thankful (Romans 1:21–23). When a person does not honor Him as God, He often allows them to begin a dangerous downward path that leads to increased mental confusion (Romans 1:22) and idolatry (Romans 1:23). If this happens and they are still not willing to recognize their error, God often turns them over to the desires of their sinful hearts, which, for some, is expressed in homosexual behavior (Romans 1:24–27). God continues to love them and wants them to return to their original created purpose of loving and honoring Him, but He withdraws His active pursuit of them so that they might be filled with the wages of their iniquity and repent. Homosexuality is a sin like any other expression of sin and can be repented of and forgiven by God. Paul, writing to the Corinthian believers, said that some of them had been

homosexuals (1 Corinthians 6:9–11). (Note: This passage is so specific that it identifies both the masculine and the feminine roles in a homosexual relationship [1 Corinthians 6:9, **homosexuals** and **sodomites**]). Paul makes a fourfold statement about these former homosexuals who are now Christians. He said, **Such were some of you, but you were washed, but you were sanctified, but you were justified** (1 Corinthians 6:11). Some of the believers in the church had been homosexuals, but they had been **washed** clean by the blood of Christ and saved by the grace of God. They had been set apart (**sanctified**) by God for His purposes. They had been saved and set free (**justified**), meaning that they now had a proper legal standing before God. Perhaps the detailed description of this passage was meant to assure the former homosexuals of God's forgiveness and remind the church that God had fully embraced them as members of His family — something the church of Jesus Christ today would do well to consider. It is important to remember that homosexuality is an immoral act and not just a feeling. Some individuals may refer to themselves as "nonpracticing homosexuals." These people are confused about God's design for their lives.

5. a. Bitterness and death (Proverbs 5:4–5). Financial ruin (Proverbs 5:10). Sorrow (Proverbs 5:11). Regret (Proverbs 5:11–13). Dishonor among the body of Christ (Proverbs 5:14).

  b. There are dozens of sexually transmitted diseases (STDs) such as gonorrhea, syphilis, herpes, and AIDS. Many of these illnesses cause a lifetime of health-related problems, including sterility, pain, and even death. Some of them are incurable.

6. a. Rueben (Genesis 49:4). King David (2 Samuel 11:1–4). Amnon (2 Samuel 13:10–15)

  b. Stay away from them (Proverbs 5:8). Don't lust after her beauty in your heart (Proverbs 6:25).

7. Don't stir up or arouse the flames of passion before there is a biblical opportunity for it to be satisfied. As the bride in the Song of Solomon experiences the burning flames of sexual passion, she realizes how powerful a force it is and warns the unmarried women in Jerusalem that they should not arouse their sexual appetites until they are married. This is good advice for believers, young and old, men and women.

8. Answers will vary but could include the following: Love gives, but lust takes. Love is concerned about fulfilling another's needs and desires; lust is consumed with fulfilling its own needs and desires. Love protects, but lust takes advantage of others. Other answers could apply.

9. a. 1. Love does not envy (1 Corinthians 13:4).
   2. Love does not parade itself or boast or brag (1 Corinthians 13:4).
   3. Love is not proud and arrogant (1 Corinthians 13:4).
   4. Love does not act rudely (1 Corinthians 13:5).
   5. Love does not seek its own (1 Corinthians 13:5).
   6. Love is not easily provoked (1 Corinthians 13:5).
   7. Love does not think evil (1 Corinthians 13:5).
   8. Love does not rejoice in sin or iniquity (1 Corinthians 13:6).
   b. 1. Love is patient (1 Corinthians 13:4).
   2. Love is kind (1 Corinthians 13:4).
   3. Love rejoices in the truth (1 Corinthians 13:6).
   4. Love bears all things (1 Corinthians 13:7).
   5. Love believes all things (1 Corinthians 13:7).
   6. Love hopes all things (1 Corinthians 13:7).
   7. Love endures all things (1 Corinthians 13:7).
   The J.B. Phillips New Testament (PHILLIPS) translation reads: "This love of which I speak is slow to lose patience—it looks for a way of being constructive. It is not possessive: it is neither anxious to impress nor does it cherish inflated ideas of its own importance. Love has good manners and does not pursue selfish advantage. It is not touchy. It does not keep account of evil or gloat over the wickedness of other people. On the contrary, it is glad with all good men when truth prevails. Love knows no limit to its endurance, no end to its trust, no fading of its hope; it can outlast anything. It is, in fact, the one thing that still stands when all else has fallen."
   c. Answers will vary.

10. a. The wife.
    b. A married couple should keep their sexual expression within the bounds of the marriage relationship. When a family drank from its own well or cistern, everyone was confident that the water was not contaminated. In the same way, it is God's will (and plan for protection against sexual contamination, including sexually transmitted diseases)

for a married couple to engage in sexual activity within the bond of marriage alone.

11. Blessed. Rejoice. Satisfy. Enraptured. Love.

12. a. A husband and wife can experience continuing sexual satisfaction within their marriage.
    b. God watches every move Christians make, and He examines every step they take. Believers are not exempt from the temporal judgment of God when they engage in immoral behavior. If someone engages in sinful conduct, he or she will eventually become ensnared and may even die as a result of their folly (Proverbs 5:23).

Lesson 7: Escaping Entrapment

1. a. The son was to see if he could get released from the commitment of putting up security to the other man as quickly as possible without violating his word (Proverbs 6:1–5).
   b. 1. The gazelle is a very fast runner, and this image conveys the speed by which the son was to escape from his folly.
      2. The use of the bird caught in a trap or snare likely meant to help the son understand the severity of the entrapment or to look for his first opportunity to escape.

2. We are responsible to others and accountable to God for the words we speak and the commitments we make even if those commitments are only verbal (Proverbs 6:1–5). Believers should not need to swear that the things they are saying at the time are true because everything they say should be true (Matthew 5:33–37). The use and misuse of oaths to verify the things we say has its source in the devil himself (Matthew 5:37).

3. The believer should realize that he has no control over the future, and he should make commitments to others in light of this important truth. When someone asks him to make a commitment that he knows he might not be able to fulfill, he ought to say to the person, "If the Lord wills …."

4. 1. The ant works diligently without supervision (Proverbs 6:7).

2. The ant prepares for future need (Proverbs 6:8).

5. They often rest or sleep when there is work to be done (Proverbs 6:9–10). Poverty will come upon them suddenly due to their indolence (Proverbs 6:11).

6. a. He winks with his eyes (Proverbs 6:13). This appears to be a reference to a signal between two people in the presence of another who is being taken advantage of. He shuffles his feet and points with his fingers (Proverbs 6:13). This tactic, often used by magicians to fool an audience, is a common tactic used by wicked people to confuse a person and communicate something other than is being said.

   b. Calamity or disaster. They will also face sudden destruction that will be so severe that they will not be able to recover.

7. a. "A proud look, a lying tongue, hands that shed innocent blood, a heart that devises wicked plans, feet that are swift in running to evil, a false witness who speaks lies, one who sows discord among brethren."

   b. Answers will vary.

8. Evil woman. Seductress. Harlot. Adulteress.

9. a. God's people are commanded to flee immorality (1 Corinthians 6:18). When an individual commits an act of immorality, he sins against God and his own body. His body is the temple of the Holy Spirit and does not belong to him. His body belongs to God because it was purchased at the time of salvation (by the blood of Jesus Christ). The believer is supposed to glorify God in his body rather than using it to lustfully gratify the desires of the flesh (1 Corinthians 6:19–20). The sexual unity of a married Christian couple should not be defiled by the introduction of a third person into that blessed union (Hebrews 13:4).

   b. Poverty (Proverbs 6:26). Divine retribution (Proverbs 6:27–29). Damage to his own soul (Proverbs 6:32). Wounds (Proverbs 6:33). Dishonor (Proverbs 6:33). Enduring reproach (Proverbs 6:33). Vengeance from the woman's husband (Proverbs 6:34).

10. Answers will vary.

Lesson 8: Highway to Hell

1. Wisdom should become the <u>apple of our eyes</u> (Proverbs 7:2). We should bind wisdom <u>on our fingers</u> and write wisdom on <u>the tablet of our hearts</u> (Proverbs 7:3). We should say to wisdom, "<u>You are my sister.</u>" (Proverbs 4). We should call wisdom <u>our nearest kin</u> (Proverbs 7:4).

2. a. 1. The father who looked out through the window and observed a young man being trapped by an immoral woman (Proverbs 7:6–7).
        2. An unspecified number of young people, all who were apparently uncommitted to God or not desirous of following His ways (Proverbs 7:7).
        3. A young man who lacked understanding who was trapped by the adulteress (Proverbs 7:8).
        4. An adulteress (Proverbs 7:10).
    b. Answers will vary but should include bars, internet "dating" sites, work, office parties, singles cruises, conventions and conferences, etc. Other answers could apply.

3. a. 1. The young man was lacking understanding (Proverbs 7:7). He was a moral accident waiting to happen.
        2. He was unwise about where he went (Proverbs 7:8).
        3. He was alone in a place where he could be easily tempted (Proverbs 7:9). There is no mention of any of the other young men making any attempt to discourage him from his sinful ways. He was not accountable to anyone else regarding his actions.
    b. 1. She is evil (Proverbs 6:24). 2. She is an immoral woman who aggressively promotes her pagan lifestyle within the community at large through deceptive speech and suggestive enticements (Proverbs 6:24–25). 3. She has a wicked heart and dresses like a harlot (Proverbs 7:10). 4. She is loud and rebellious (Proverbs 7:11). 5. She does not stay at home (Proverbs 7:11–12). 6. She actively hunts for her sexual victims (Proverbs 7:13). 7. She is pretentious in her religious devotion (Proverbs 7:14). 8. She is clamorous (Proverbs 9:13). 9. She is overt about her immoral behavior (Proverbs 9:14–17).

4. a. Answers will vary.
    b. The individual should be affirmed for his or her courage to share the

problem with you. You should tell the individual that any personal information they shared with you will not be shared with anyone else. You should ask the individual what you can do to help him. You should also ask the individual how he or she sees the problem in relationship to God and His Word. You should consider meeting with him regularly for prayer, Bible study, and accountability. If you do not feel you are the right person to help him or her, you should consider introducing him to your pastor or another trustworthy Christian (man with another man, woman with another woman) who can help him gain victory over the problem.

5. a. Lust is impatient, but love is patient (1 Corinthians 13:4). Lust is often rude and boorish, but love is kind (1 Corinthians 13:4). Lust flaunts itself and is proud of its sensuality, but love does not parade itself and is not arrogant (1 Corinthians 13:4). Lust often expresses itself rudely, but love is not rude (1 Corinthians 13:5). Lust focuses on human emotion and is often easily offended, but love is not easily provoked (1 Corinthians 13:5). Lust seeks to take advantage of others, but love thinks no evil (1 Corinthians 13:5). Lust endures very little, but love bears and endures all things (1 Corinthians 13:7).

    b. Answers will vary.

6. a. 1. A fool to the correction of the stocks (Proverbs 7:22). 2. As a bird hastens to the snare (Proverbs 7:23). 3. She has cast down many wounded (Proverbs 7:26). 4. Her house is the way to the grave (Proverbs 7:27). 5. Descending to the chambers of death (Proverbs 7:27).

    b. Answers will vary.

7. Christians can learn to stand up for truth within all aspects of society. They can maintain sexual purity in their own lives and educate their children in all the ways of the Lord, including God's sexual standards. They can vote for local, state, and national officials who support God's standard of moral behavior. They can voice their opinion in love at school board and other meetings. Other answers could apply.

8. a. 1. Sexual attraction is a powerful force. The bride in Song of Solomon warns against awaking passion before it has an opportunity to

rightfully express itself in a marriage (Song of Solomon 2:7; 3:5; 5:8; 8:4).

    2. In a culture when God's Word is not honored, the norm is sexual expression and immoral behavior. Christians often accept the world's values rather than hold fast to God's standard of moral behavior. Other answers could apply.

  b. Answers will vary.

Lesson 9: In Wisdom's Own Words

1. Wisdom calls to anyone who will listen (Proverbs 8:2–3) but makes a special appeal to the simple and to fools (Proverbs 8:5).

2. a. The Word of God.
  b. 1. The believer must learn the Bible ("He who has My commandments …," John 14:21).
     2. The believer must obey the Bible ("… and keeps them," John 14:21).

3. Excellent things. (Proverbs 8:6). Right things. (Proverbs 8:6). Truth. (Proverbs 8:7). Righteousness. (Proverbs 8:8). Plain. (Proverbs 8:9). Right. (Proverbs 8:9). Better than rubies. (Proverbs 8:11). All things … cannot be compared with her. (Proverbs 8:11).

4. a. Answers will vary, but they could include the following: 1. The believer should consider making a commitment to study the Bible every day. 2. The believer should consider becoming an active part of a Bible-believing church where God's Word is taught accurately and lovingly and applied to their lives. Other answers could apply.
  b. A church should make certain that only sound biblical teaching is offered in the ministries of the church. They should look closely at the curriculum that is used in all levels of their Christian education. A church should also choose only biblically qualified individuals to lead the church. A church should pray for guidance, wisdom and protection of the ministry. Other answers could apply.

5. a. Leaders need wisdom to help them listen and understand others.

Leaders can be tempted to "jump to conclusions" and make decisions that harm others. Leaders need wisdom to help them think clearly so they make wise decisions, which will benefit their followers and maximize the skills and potential of those who responsible to them. If a leader consistently makes unwise decisions, those who are following him will become frustrated and lose heart. Other answers could apply.

   b. Answers will vary.

6. a. 1. God will demonstrate His abundant love to those who love Him (Proverbs 8:17).

          2. If they diligently seek God, they will find Him (Proverbs 8:17; Matthew 7:7–8).

          3. If they ask for wisdom, God will give it to them generously (James 1:5).

   b. God will provide enduring riches, honor, righteousness, and a divine fruit that is better than fine gold (Proverbs 8:18–19). God walks in the way of the righteous (a figure of speech to show that He observes what men are doing) to determine who is worthy to inherit wealth and have their treasuries filled (Proverbs 8:20–21). Financial blessing is not guaranteed to those who live according to His plan. Those who preach a "prosperity gospel" fail to realize that God chose many mighty saints (John the Baptist, Paul, the Macedonian believers) who were poor in earthly wealth but rich in faith and blessed in eternity (Hebrews 11:36–39).

7. Believers should use the earth but not abuse it. It is a gift from God, and believers are commanded to be good stewards of the gifts that God allows them to use.

8. a. The builder who built his house on the rock is compared to the man who builds his life on the Word of God. He hears and obeys the Word of God. When the winds of adversity come (rain, floods, winds), his life does not falter (Matthew 7:24–25). The builder who builds his house on the sand is compared to a man who rejects the Word of God (he hears the Word but does not obey it) and lives by human reason. His life is shattered when adversity comes.

   b. At times of adversity.

   c. Answers will vary.

9. The Word of God did not help the Israelites during the time of the Exodus because they were not willing to trust God for what He said.

10. a, b, c, d, e. Answers will vary.

11. Answers will vary.

Lesson 10: Wisdom's Rewards

1. a. She invites the simple and the ones who lack understanding (Proverbs 9:3–4).
    b. She offers to serve them wisdom so they can live skillfully with understanding.

2. a. A scoffer hates those who instruct him and those who attempt to do so only harm themselves (Proverbs 9:7–8a). A scoffer doesn't listen to those who instruct or correct him (Proverbs 13:1). A scoffer doesn't like those who correct him (Proverbs 15:12) because he is proud and arrogant (Proverbs 21:24).
    b. A wise man loves those who correct him, and he receives the instruction and gains wisdom (Proverbs 9:8–9).
    c. Answers will vary.

3. a. Connecting Proverb.
    b. 1. Correct   Rebukes.
        2. Scoffer   Wicked man.
        3. Gets shame (NIV" insult") Harms himself

4. 1. They do not want their sins to be exposed (John 3:19–20).
    2. Satan has blinded the minds of all unsaved people. Only Christ can open their hearts and minds (2 Corinthians 4:4).

5. a. Their desires are contrary to God's will for their lives. Instead of yielding their hearts and minds to God, they reject the truth and find religious teachers who tell them what they want to hear rather than what they need to hear.
    b. Timothy was to keep preaching the Word of God (2 Timothy 4:2). He

was to do it with courage, concern, and patience. He was to do it until God redirected his steps or removed him from the ministry, either by reassignment or death.

6. Answers will vary.

7. Answers will vary.

8. a. Answers will vary. The fear of the Lord is reverential awe that causes a believer to put away all evil from his life and motivates him to walk in God's ways, love Him, and serve Him with all his heart and soul.
   b. Answers will vary.
   c. Fear comes from the devil. The cure for fear is to acknowledge the abiding presence of the Lord (Isaiah 41:10), knowing that He is our helper (Isaiah 41:13). We must learn to actively wait on the Lord and trust Him to bring into our lives only what He divinely ordains for His glory. He created us, redeemed us, and He knows us intimately (Isaiah 43:1). We can trust Him.

9. Answers will vary.

10. Answers will vary.

FINAL EXAM

Every person will eventually stand before God in judgment—the final exam. The Bible says, **And it is appointed for men to die once, but after this the judgment** (Hebrews 9:27).

May I ask you a question? *If you died today, do you know for certain you would go to heaven?* I did not ask if you're religious or a church member, nor did I ask if you've had some encounter with God—a meaningful spiritual experience. I didn't even ask if you believe in God or angels or if you're trying to live a good life. The question I *am* asking is this: *If you died today, do you know for certain you would go to heaven?*

When you die, you will stand alone before God in judgment. You'll either be saved for all eternity, or you will be separated from God for all eternity in what the Bible calls the lake of fire (Romans 14:12; Revelation 20:11–15). Tragically, many religious people who believe in God are not going to be accepted by Him when they die.

> **Many will say to Me in that day, "Lord, Lord, have we not prophesied in Your name, cast out demons in Your name, and done many wonders in Your name?" And then I will declare to them, "I never knew you; depart from Me, you who practice lawlessness!"** (Matthew 7:22–23)

God loves you and wants you to go to heaven (John 3:16; 2 Peter 3:9). If you are not sure where you'll spend eternity, you are not prepared to meet God. God wants you to know for certain that you will go to heaven.

> **Behold, now is the accepted time; behold, now is the day of salvation.** (2 Corinthians 6:2)

The words **behold** and **now** are repeated because God wants you to know that you can be saved today. You do not need to hear those terrible words, **Depart from Me ....** Isn't that great news?

Jesus himself said, **You must be born again** (John 3:7). These aren't the words of a pastor, a church, or a particular denomination. They're the words of Jesus Christ himself. You *must* be born again (saved from eternal damnation) before you die; otherwise, it will be too late when you die! You can know for certain today that God will accept you into heaven when you die.

*These things I have written to you who believe in the name of the Son of God, that you may **know** that you have eternal life.*

(1 John 5:13)

The phrase **you may know** means that you can know for certain before you die that you will go to heaven. To be born again, you must understand and accept four essential spiritual truths. These truths are right from the Bible, so you know you can trust them—they are not man-made religious traditions. Now, let's consider these four essential spiritual truths.

Essential Spiritual Truth

#1

The Bible teaches that you are a sinner and separated from God.

No one is righteous in God's eyes. To be righteous means to be totally without sin, not even a single act.

There is none righteous, no, not one;
There is none who understands;
There is none who seeks after God.
They have all turned aside;
They have together become unprofitable;
There is none who does good, no, not one.
(Romans 3:10–12)

...for all have sinned and fall short of the glory of God.
(Romans 3:23)

Look at the words God uses to show that all men are sinners—**none, not one, all turned aside, not one**. God is making a point: all of us are sinners. No one is good (perfectly without sin) in His sight. The reason is sin.

Have you ever lied, lusted, hated someone, stolen anything, or taken God's name in vain, even once? These are all sins.

Are you willing to admit to God that you are a sinner? If so, then tell Him right now you have sinned. You can say the words in your heart or aloud—it doesn't matter which—but be honest with God. Now check the box if you have just admitted you are a sinner.

☐ God, I admit I am a sinner in Your eyes.

Spiritual Death

Eternal Life

Now, let's look at the second essential spiritual truth.

Essential Spiritual Truth

#2

The Bible teaches that you cannot save yourself or earn your way to heaven.

Man's sin is a very serious problem in the eyes of God. Your sin separates you from God, both now and for all eternity—unless you are born again.

For the wages of sin is death.
(Romans 6:23)

And you He made alive, who were dead in trespasses and sins.
(Ephesians 2:1)

Wages are a payment a person earns by what he or she has done. Your sin has earned you the wages of death, which means separation from God. If you die never having been born again, you will be separated from God after death.

You cannot save yourself or purchase your entrance into heaven. The Bible says that man is **not redeemed with corruptible things, like silver or gold** (1 Peter 1:18). If you owned all the money in the world, you still could not buy your entrance into heaven. Neither can you buy your way into heaven with good works.

For by grace you have been saved through faith, and that not of yourselves; it is the gift of God, not of works, lest anyone should boast. (Ephesians 2:8–9)

The Bible says salvation is **not of yourselves**. It is **not of works, lest anyone should boast**. Salvation from eternal judgment cannot be earned by doing good works; it is a gift of God. There is nothing you can do to purchase your way into heaven because you are already unrighteous in God's eyes.

If you understand you cannot save yourself, then tell God right now that you are a sinner, separated from Him, and you cannot save yourself. Check the box below if you have just done that.

☐ God, I admit that I am separated from You because of my sin. I realize that I cannot save myself.

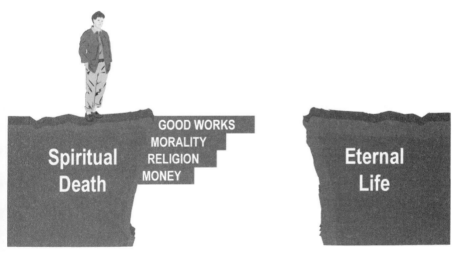

Now, let's look at the third essential spiritual truth.

Essential Spiritual Truth

#3

The Bible teaches that Jesus Christ died on the cross to pay the complete penalty for your sin and to purchase a place in heaven for you.

Jesus Christ, the sinless Son of God, lived a perfect life, died on the cross, and rose from the dead to pay the penalty for your sin and purchase a place in heaven for you. He died on the cross on your behalf, in your place, as your substitute, so you do not have to go to hell. Jesus Christ is the only acceptable substitute for your sin.

For He [God, the Father] made Him [Jesus] who knew [committed] no sin to be sin for us, that we might become the righteousness of God in Him.
(2 Corinthians 5:21)

I [Jesus] am the way, the truth, and the life. No one comes to the Father except through Me.
(John 14:6)

Nor is there salvation in any other, for there is no other name under heaven given among men by which we must be saved.
(Acts 4:12)

Jesus Christ is your only hope and means of salvation. Because you are a sinner, you cannot pay for your sins, but Jesus paid the penalty for your sins by dying on the cross in your place. Friend, there is salvation in no one else—not angels, not some religious leader, not even your religious good works. No religious act such as baptism, confirmation, or joining a church can save you. There is no other way, no other name that can save you. Only Jesus Christ can save you. You must be saved by accepting Jesus Christ's substitutionary sacrifice for your sins, or you will be lost forever.

Do you see clearly that Jesus Christ is the only way to God in heaven? If you understand this truth, tell God that you understand, and check the box below.

☐ God, I understand that Jesus Christ died to pay the penalty for my sin. I understand that His death on the cross was the only acceptable sacrifice for my sin.

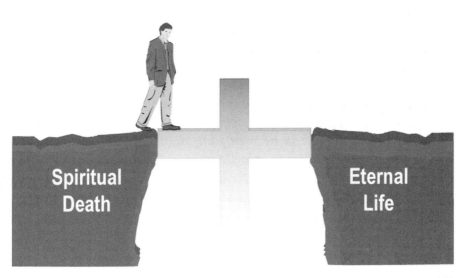

Spiritual Death

Eternal Life

Essential Spiritual Truth

#4

By faith, you must trust in Jesus Christ alone for eternal life and call upon Him to be your Savior and Lord.

Many religious people admit they have sinned. They believe Jesus Christ died for the sins of the world, but they are not saved. Why? Thousands of moral, religious people have never completely placed their faith in Jesus Christ *alone* for eternal life. They think they must believe in Jesus Christ as a real person and do good works to earn their way to heaven. They are not trusting Jesus Christ alone. To be saved, you must trust in Jesus Christ *alone* for eternal life. Look what the Bible teaches about trusting Jesus Christ alone for salvation.

> *Believe on the Lord Jesus Christ, and you will be saved.*
> (Acts 16:31)

> *...that if you confess with your mouth the Lord Jesus and believe in your heart that God has raised Him from the dead, you will be saved. For with the heart one believes unto righteousness, and with the mouth confession is made unto salvation.... For there is no distinction between Jew and Greek, for the same Lord over all is rich to all who call upon Him. For "whoever calls on the name of the Lord shall be saved.*
> (Romans 10:9–10, 12–13)

Do you see what God is saying? To be saved or born again, you must trust Jesus Christ *alone* for eternal life. Jesus Christ paid for your complete salvation. Jesus said, **It is finished!** (John 19:30). Jesus paid for your salvation completely when He shed His blood on the cross for your sin.

If you believe that God resurrected Jesus Christ (proving God's acceptance of Jesus as a worthy sacrifice for man's sin) and you are willing to confess Jesus Christ as your Savior and Lord (master of your life), you will be saved.

Friend, right now God is offering you the greatest gift in the world. God wants to give you the *gift* of eternal life, the *gift* of His complete forgiveness for all your sins, and the *gift* of His unconditional acceptance into heaven when you die. Will you accept His free gift now, right where you are?

Are you unsure how to receive the gift of eternal life? Let me help you. Do you remember that I said you needed to understand and accept four essential spiritual truths? First, you admitted you are a sinner. Second, you admitted you were separated from God because of your sin and you could not save yourself. Third, you realized that Jesus Christ is the only way to heaven—no other name can save you.

Now, you must trust that Jesus Christ died once and for all to save your lost soul. Just take God at His word—He will not lie to you! This is the kind of simple faith you need to be saved. If you would like to be saved right now, right where you are, offer this prayer of simple faith to God. Remember, the words must come from your heart.

God, I am a sinner and deserve to go to hell. Thank You, Jesus, for dying on the cross for me and for purchasing a place in heaven for me. I believe You are the Son of God and You are able to save me right now. Please forgive me for my sin and take me to heaven when I die. I invite You into my life as Savior and Lord, and I trust You alone for eternal life. Thank You for giving me the gift of eternal life. Amen.

If, in the best way you know how, you trusted Jesus Christ alone to save you, then God just saved you. He said in His Holy Word, *But as many as received Him, to them He gave the right to become the children of God* (John 1:12). It's that simple. God just gave you the gift of eternal life by faith. You have just been born again, according to the Bible.

You will not come into eternal judgment, and you will not perish in the lake of fire—you are saved forever! Read this verse carefully and let it sink into your heart.

> *Most assuredly, I say to you, he who hears My word and believes in Him who sent Me has everlasting life, and shall not come into judgment, but has passed from death into life.*
> (John 5:24)

Now, let me ask you a few more questions.

According to God's holy Word (John 5:24), not your feelings, what kind of life did God just give you? _____

What two words did God say at the beginning of the verse to assure you that He is not lying to you? _____ _____

Are you going to come into eternal judgment? ☐ YES ☐ NO

Have you passed from spiritual death into life? ☐ YES ☐ NO

Friend, you've just been born again. You just became a child of God.

To help you grow in your new Christian life, we would like to send you some Bible study materials. To receive these helpful materials free of charge, e-mail your request to **info@LamplightersUSA.org.**

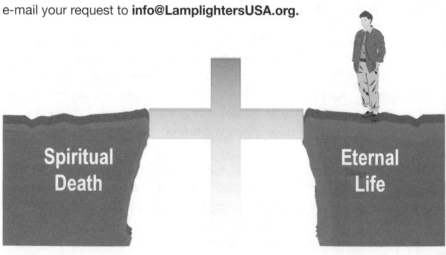

Spiritual Death

Eternal Life

APPENDIX

LEVEL 1 (BASIC TRAINING)
STUDENT WORKBOOK

To begin, familiarize yourself with the Lamplighters' *Leadership Training and Development Process* (see graphic on page 116). Notice there are two circles: a smaller, inner circle and a larger, outer circle. The inner circle shows the sequence of weekly meetings beginning with an Open House, followed by an 8–14 week study, and concluding with a clear presentation of the gospel (Final Exam). The outer circle shows the sequence of the Intentional Discipleship training process (Leading Studies, Training Leaders, Multiplying Groups). As participants are transformed by God's Word, they're invited into a discipleship training process that equips them in every aspect of the intentional disciple-making ministry.

The Level 1 training (Basic Training) is *free*, and the training focuses on two key aspects of the training: 1) how to prepare a life-changing Bible study (ST-A-R-T) and 2) how to lead a life-changing Bible study (10 commandments). The training takes approximately 60 minutes to complete, and you complete it as an individual or collectively as a small group (preferred method) by inserting an extra week between the Final Exam and the Open House.

To begin your training, go to www.LamplightersUSA.org to register yourself or your group. A Lamplighters' Certified Trainer will guide you through the entire Level 1 training process. After you have completed the training, you can review as many times as you like.

When you have completed the Level 1 training, please consider completing the Level 2 (Advanced) training. Level 2 training will equip you to reach more people for Christ by learning how to train new leaders and by showing you how to multiply groups. You can register for additional training at www. LamplightersUSA.org.

Intentional Discipleship
Training & Development Process

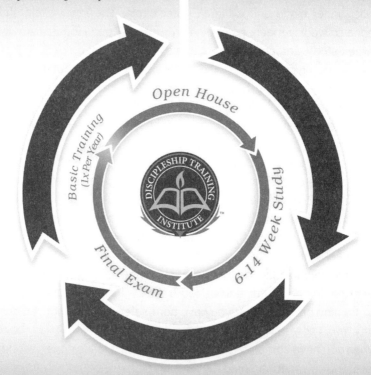

3. Multiplying Groups

The "5 Steps" for Starting
New Groups
The Audio Training Library (ATL)
The Importance of the Open House

1. Leading Studies

ST-A-R-T
10 Commandments
Solving All Group Problems

Open House

Basic Training
(1x Per Year)

6-14 Week Study

Final Exam

2. Training Leaders

Four-fold ministry of a leader   The 2P's for recruiting new leaders
The Three Diagnostic Questions   The three stages of leadership training

How to Prepare a Life-Changing Bible Study

ST-A-R-T

Step 1: _____ and _____.

    Pray specifically for the group members and yourself as you study God's Word. Ask God (_____) to give each group member a rich time of personal Bible study, and thank (_____) God for giving you a desire to invest in the spiritual advancement of each other.

Step 2: _____ the _____.

    Answer the questions in the weekly lessons without looking at the _____ _____.

Step 3: _____and _____.

    Review the Leader's Guide, and _____ every truth you missed when you originally did your lesson. Record the answers you missed with a _____ _____ so you'll know what you missed.

Step 4: _____ _____.

    Calculate the specific amount of time _____ _____ to spend on each question and write the start time next to each one in the _____ using a _____.

How to Lead a Life-Changing Bible Study

10 COMMANDMENTS

1	2	3
4	5	6
7	8	9
10		

Lamplighters' 10 Commandments are proven small group leadership principles that have been used successfully to train hundreds of believers to lead life-changing, intentional discipleship Bible studies.

Essential Principles for Leading Intentional Discipleship Bible Studies

1. The 1st Commandment: The _____ Rule.
The Leader-Trainer should be in the room _____ minutes before the class begins.

2. The 2nd Commandment: The _____-_____ Rule.
Train the group that it is okay to _____, but they should never be _____.

3. The 3rd Commandment: The _____ Rule.
_____, _____, _____ ask for _____ to _____ the _____, _____, and _____ the questions. The Leader-Trainer, however, should always _____ the questions to control the _____ of the study.

4. The 4th Commandment: The ____:____ Rule.
_____ the Bible study on time and _____ the study on time _____ _____. No exceptions!

5. The 5th Commandment: The _____ Rule.
Train the group participants to _____ on God's Word for answers to life's questions.

1	2	3
4 **59:59**	5	6
7	8	9
	10	

6. The 6th Commandment: The _____ Rule.
   Deliberately and progressively _____ _____ participants into the
   group discussion over a period of time.

7. The 7th Commandment: The _____ _____ Rule.
   _____ the participants to get _____ the answers to the
   questions, not just _____ or _____ ones.

8. The 8th Commandment: The _____ Rule.
   _____ the group discussion so you _____ the
   lesson _____ _____ and give each question _____
   _____.

9. The 9th Commandment: The _____-_____ Rule.
   Don't let the group members talk about _____
   _____, _____ _____, or
   _____ _____.

10. The 10th Commandment: The _____ Rule.
    _____ God to change lives, including _____.

Choose your next study from any of the following titles:

- Joshua 1-9
- Joshua 10-24
- Judges 1-10
- Judges 11-21
- Ruth/Esther
- Jonah/Habakkuk
- Nehemiah
- Proverbs 1-9
- Proverbs 10-31
- Ecclesiastes
- John 1-11
- John 12-21
- Acts 1-12
- Acts 13-28

- Romans 1-8
- Romans 9-16
- Galatians
- Ephesians
- Philippians
- Colossians
- 1 & 2 Thessalonians
- 1 Timothy
- 2 Timothy
- Titus/Philemon
- Hebrews
- James
- 1 Peter
- 2 Peter/Jude

Additional Bible studies and sample lessons are available online.

For audio introductions on all Bible studies, visit us online at www.Lamplightersusa.org.

Looking to begin a new group?
The Lamplighters Starter Kit includes:

- 8 James Bible Study Guides
  (students purchase their own books)
- 25 Welcome Booklets
- 25 Table Tents
- 25 Bible Book Locator Bookmarks
- 50 Final Exam Tracts
- 50 Invitation Cards

For a current listing of live and online discipleship training
events, or to register for discipleship training, go to
www.LamplightersUSA.org/training.

Become a Certified Disciple-Maker

Discipleship Training Institute

Certificate of Completion

This is to certify that _____

has successfully completed the requirements of the

_____ course.

_____   _____

Date   President

Training Courses Available:

- Leader-Trainer
- Discipleship Coach
- Discipleship Director

Contact the Discipleship Training Institute for more information (800-507-9516).

The Discipleship Training Institute is a ministry of Lamplighters International.